SMOKE SIGNALS
The Eleven Unwritten Rules of Negotiation

GEORGE KISER

© 2015 George Kiser

All Rights Reserved.

No part of this publication may be reproduced, stored in a retrieval system, or transmitted, in any form or by any means, electronic, mechanical, photocopying, recording, or otherwise, without the written permission of the author.

First published by Dog Ear Publishing
4011 Vincennes Rd
Indianapolis, IN 46268
www.dogearpublishing.net

ISBN: 978-1-4575-4049-3

This book is printed on acid-free paper.

Printed in the United States of America

TABLE OF CONTENTS

CHAPTER 1	The Basics	3
CHAPTER 2	The Opening Salvo	10
CHAPTER 3	The Unspoken Rules of Ettiquette	19
CHAPTER 4	Recap Before the 11 Rules	23
CHAPTER 5	Rule Number I, Be Realistic	26
CHAPTER 6	Rule Number II, Set a Goal	33
CHAPTER 7	Rule Number III, What is Your Bottom Line?	36
CHAPTER 8	Rule Number IV, Your Composure; Keep it	40
CHAPTER 9	Rule Number V, Be Able to Read the Smoke Signals from the Other Side	47
CHAPTER 10	Rule Number VI, Learn to Send Your Own Smoke Signals	61
CHAPTER 11	Rule Number VII, The Rule of ½ - Split the Difference	74
CHAPTER 12	Rule Number VIII, Be Willing to Walk Away	79
CHAPTER 13	Rule Number IX, Don't be Penny Wise and Pound Foolish	83
CHAPTER 14	Rule Number X, Never Say Never – Almost	88
CHAPTER 15	Rule Number XI, Saving Face	93
CHAPTER 16	The Thrill of Victory and the Agony of Defeat	96

FOREWORD AND THANKS

I learn something each time I negotiate. I have negotiated literally hundreds of civil lawsuits, bought a few cars, houses and negotiated contracts over the last 20-plus years. I did not wake up one day and know the unwritten rules of negotiation. I did not all of a sudden know what to do or say when trying to settle a lawsuit or negotiate a contract. I have been lucky to have been on the other side of some really, really good negotiators.

So thank you to all those who have so generously participated in my training. I really have learned by doing, and often learned by doing things wrong. I also have learned by watching what other people have done right.

I mention later in this book that my dad could have written these rules, and he certainly could have. So could many others who I know and have observed, many of whom are my partners at HeplerBroom LLC (the best civil defense firm I know). Civil lawyers, I think, are uniquely qualified to talk about negotiation because they have the opportunity to do a lot of it. The rules in this book, though, are not unique to lawyers. I hope they help make the experience of buying your new car or the home of your dreams a little less daunting.

INTRODUCTION

"I wish there was a book telling me how to negotiate a lease, or help me buy a car! I always feel like I get taken advantage of when I buy a car; I simply don't know how to wrestle the salesman down to a comfortable price. So I always feel like I pay too much."

OK, I never said that and no one ever actually told me that. If someone had confessed that to me, it would have made a great introductory paragraph for a book on how to negotiate. But I know that there are people who feel this way and no one has to. There are some very simple rules that will help everyone buy that car, or house or negotiate a lease or even a pay-check. I know they are simple because I am not an intellectual.

I did not study psychology in college nor am I psychic, able to read people's minds and determine just where their breaking point is. I am not that person who always seems to finagle the best deal from the House of Cadillac and then brags to the neighbors about the deal I got. I have, though, negotiated several major civil lawsuits involving hundreds of thousands of dollars. I have negotiated on behalf of those who sued others for money and for those who wanted to keep as much of their own as possible. I have walked away smiling sometimes, and depressed and unsatisfied on other occasions. And I have done the ordinary things we all fret; bought cars, sold houses and talked money with the boss.

This book is really about my observations and experiences. It is a compilation of what to do right when you are in the negotiation boat. It does not represent everything there is to know about how to negotiate. But it is an easily understood guide to something that we all take for granted, but really don't know much about or think much about.

I do think that the most common negotiation in which any of us will ever participate is buying a car. Thus, this book is based on the notion that I am going to give you some rules to use when buying your next new or used car. The principles involved, however, are applicable to virtually any negotiation. They also offer real insight about how the good negotiators approach their objective.

There are "Idiots Guides" to almost everything. This is not one of them. I am not going to define the word "negotiation" or "objective." The rules in this book are simple but they are not that rudimentary. Yet, this is not the advanced manual either. Hopefully, this book will provide insight into how a negotiation progresses, or how it should progress, and gives you some advanced suggestions to use when you are inevitably in the position to be negotiating for something you want or need. I hope it helps you buy your next car, or home, negotiate a contract or settle a lawsuit.

CHAPTER 1

THE BASICS

Real estate moguls put together deals every day. Capital management companies, like that run by T. Boone Pickens, buy and sell companies. Construction companies bid on contracts to build, rebuild and repair homes or businesses. Unions negotiate new employment contracts. Greedy plaintiff attorneys settle their clients' claims with those big, bad insurance companies. You and I buy and sell cars.

What do each of these and so many other situations have in common? They involve negotiating, bickering or bartering. All of them involve the exchange of one thing or more for others; usually, but not always money at least. The circumstances of a big real estate deal differ from the settlement of a small lawsuit only in degree and what is exchanged. All of these situations share common strategies and rules.

Not all negotiations are as complex as a real estate transaction or buying a company. All start with an initial price or bid. The more complex and involved the deals are, the more little things that can be bartered, and the more things that can go wrong. I remember looking at those big stereo systems of the 1980s and all of the buttons and lights on each of the different, separate components. Too much stuff to go wrong, people complained. That's always the case, isn't it?

Those of us who have had children know negotiation intrinsically. In fact, haven't we all participated? Kids negotiate early and often. They trade good behavior for TV time, time with their friends, food, food and food. Then, as they get older, they want to trade whatever they can for the car, the car, the car. Most are good at it; very good at it. Their approach is pretty simple. Start at the moon, the absolute best that they could hope to obtain or want and simply work their way down until their parents agree. Technically, I am not sure that they have a bottom line, but it works really well for them doesn't it? They have a plan, they have a goal to do as much of something or get as big a slice of pizza as they can and they whine, whimper and bargain whatever they can until they get it. Actually, that is not a bad strategy at all. But as we get older, we seem to lose our will or maybe we become less forceful. And most grown-up negotiations are a little more involved.

Thus, the strategies in this book are a little above our children's level. There are people who negotiate, or barter, for a living. The difference between them and us is practice, and knowledge of a few rules or strategies to get what they want. That and the stakes are often higher for the professional negotiator. Their secrets, their rules, are applicable to virtually every negotiation that we may find ourselves in.

In any negotiation you need to have a goal. What do you want and what are you willing to give up to get it? You need a plan. How are you going to start out, what are you going to do to give yourself the best chance to obtain your goal. And you need a plan B. What are you going to do when things go sour?

The Imbalance of Power

Before we start looking at our goals or plans, a word about the balance of power – it's never equal. Have you ever negotiated the price you pay for your home owners' insurance or automobile insurance? I thought not. Why not? The reason is that in the insurance market, the companies are able to tell you that their price is take it or leave it. You can pay less for that State Farm or Allstate car policy, but you will have to drop coverages to do it. I can pretty much guarantee you that you couldn't walk into your agent's office and negotiate the price that you are willing to pay for a set of coverage. I do not recommend utilizing the strategies in this book to try and lower the cost of liability insurance; it won't work.

While there certainly is competition among insurers for your dollar, the power to dictate their fee for a particular coverage is all theirs. What they charge is part actuarial, part underwriting and part market competition with other companies. It is not about you or your power of persuasion or knowledge. You have nothing to offer the company, so it is take it or leave it. So if you bought this book hoping to be armed for your next visit with your automobile insurance agent, bad news. Fortunately, I don't think many of you did so.

Insurance isn't the only thing that is non-negotiable out there. I once represented a major municipal corporation (that will remain nameless) and was put in charge of all of their contracts. I drafted and re-drafted as many as I could to make the terms more favorable to the government entity. My client got everything in writing. I quickly realized that every vendor wanted to do business with the government. There were plenty of companies that would do the work if any favored soul refused.

So I enacted a very successful policy; my client's terms were simply not-negotiable, take it or leave it. Why? Because I could. The government had the power to dictate this result. If a company refused to sign the contract with all of its terms and conditions, there were plenty of willing replacements who would.

The lesson here is simple. Power is almost never equal. All sides have varying degrees of it, some always seem to have more of it than others. That's not an outrage, that's the way it has always been. I suspect that when cavemen started to barter, those with access to wood, or food or items of clothing (especially for those ugly cave people who needed covering up) had more power when bartering. Life is never quite fair, is it? On the other hand, we all do have some power in a negotiation. We have something that someone else wants. It's not always about money, either. Information, knowledge and supply and demand create power beyond the almighty dollar.

We know that at the end of the Second World War the cease fire agreement was signed on the USS Missouri. A long, bloody negotiation; but a negotiation nonetheless. The balance of power shifted in favor of the Allies because they won the battles on the war field. It brought the Axis to the bargaining table and surrender.

Buying a home or negotiating a contract to build a skyscraper is not war. One party does not surrender at the end and sign a cease fire agreement because they have to. But the power one side has over the other does matter and it can change. If a seller has to close and use the money from the sale in order to buy another home he or she has already agreed to buy, they have less power. They have to be willing to negotiate – give in – so they can sell their home.

If a real estate magnate needs to break ground to keep favorable tax financing or comply with his investor's requirements, the magnate is at a disadvantage when negotiating with the general contractor.

Make it a point to find out what pressures the other side might be under. Make it a point to know your own limitations and pressure. If you are buying a home and need to be settled in by July to start a job or get your kids in school for the new year, you may not be in a position to try and buy that home for another five or ten thousand less; you run the risk that the seller will reject your offer and leave you homeless. Power doesn't depend solely on money, it is a function of circumstance and need more than anything else.

In this book, I want to focus on a relatively simple "transaction" or situation that almost all of us will face, but so many of us dread: Buying a car. I saw a commercial the other day that chronicled a boy wonder who healed the sick at a young age, built skyscrapers and became a very successful businessman. Then, as the story goes, he froze when he had to negotiate to buy his first car! Really! Is it that hard? Is it the new fear, replacing public speaking and death as the most dreaded events in ones' life? I hope that you answer that question with a resounding "no", after reading this book, of course.

I do think that there are some people who would like you to think that negotiating to buy a car is difficult, so they can make it very simple for you; as simple as I made it for those vendors dealing with my municipal government client. Don't believe their commercials. Read on. Buying a car, selling a car, negotiating the sale or purchase of a home, settling an insurance claim, negotiating that contract to remodel your home, building a pool or negotiating that contract for your business are not difficult. But they do share one thing in common; language. There is a language that is spoken, but not written down, by those who do this thing all the time. Master the language, send the right signals and you won't dread negotiation. Read on.

The Set Up

As you have probably guessed, we could talk about so many different negotiation scenarios that there simply isn't room in this book to list them all. Think of all of the times that you negotiate to buy something, or trade something in. From building a shopping center to remodeling your basement, we all negotiate something. In fact, as I said, some of the best negotiators are children. By the time we grow up, though, some of us outgrow our gift. Maybe it just isn't taught, maybe it's not encouraged. Maybe it doesn't become necessary any more, and that's our faults, parents. For whatever reason, some of us simply don't speak the language anymore.

Yet, almost all of us will do that one thing that requires some modicum of negotiation. We will buy a car at some point in our lives, and most of us will do so on many occasions. At some point, we will be sitting in the car dealership bickering over the final price. It's an American tradition! We love our cars, God bless us.

So for this book and the "language of negotiation", in order to demonstrate how to send "smoke signals" to the other side, I will use the ordinary purchase of a new car, a Ford, as an example. We will follow a nice, middle aged couple (in their 40's, though. That is really young isn't it?) with a couple of kids.

Dana Meriweather is a pleasant young (ahem, middle aged) woman who is in the market for an SUV. She and her husband, Ted Meriweather, have scoured the new car ads in the newspaper of the city in which they live; your city for purposes of this book. They have done their homework. They went to various dealers taking test drives, bringing their two kids with them. Of course, Holly Terror Meriweather just wants a pink car. Her brother, Bam (not Bam Bam, this is a serious book), wants one that will out run the local authorities, and looks good on a date.

They also have researched potential vehicles on the internet. They looked at sites that compared service records, reliability, resale values and listed the options available on each SUV. They looked at internet sites that purported to reveal how much of a discount off of the sticker prices the dealers in their area were likely to offer. After all of this legwork and dreaming, they found the SUV that they wanted to buy. Dana and Ted scoured the new SUV dealers to find the specific SUV that they wanted to try and buy. Dana wanted to be the lead negotiator – she feared Ted's timidity would not hold up well against those mean car salesmen. She couldn't tell Ted that though, fearing he would pout. In any event, they went to the dealership together, but Dana did most of the talking. We will look at Dana's attempt to buy that Ford.

ACME Ford is located right on the West side of the city in an area known as "Auto Row". There are no less than ten new car dealerships within this three mile stretch of one of the main arteries in town. If you needed a new car, surely you could find one among these large dealerships. ACME Ford is big; really big. The president of the Ford Motor Company pretended to buy his car here once as a publicity stunt. Always one of the top sales dealerships in the country, ACME executives are actually upset when they can't close a deal. Salesmen have been fired for not making a sale, despite their overall sales records. That is not something they trumpet to their potential customers, however.

Dana and Ted will talk with one of ACME's best. Jerry Wholesale is a salesman extraordinaire. He lives and breathes the virtues of the Ford Motor Company. Just like he did Chevrolet and Dodge when he sold for rival dealers. Those cars aren't so great anymore. He knows that if he doesn't get that promotion to management soon, he may go foreign; VW to start, work his way up to Volvo or Audi. He knows the car business, he knows the cars he sells and he likes them. He knows how to try and talk people into buying from him. But like Dana, he could learn a little about the unwritten rules of negotiation.

The car that Dana and Ted want to buy is a Ford Edge SUV. It has a price tag of $41,500. The Edge is the perfect match of performance, style and utility for their active family of four. They can haul the kids to soccer games, haul the Christmas gifts to granny's and take it out for a nice dinner and not be too ashamed to use the valet. They do worry about all that room in the back for either kid's dating habits, but that is a subject for a whole other book. For now, that's all you need to know. So before we learn the 11 rules of negotiation, we need to start the process.

CHAPTER 2

THE OPENING SALVO

Admittedly, the first question Dana asks, after she and Ted fall in love with a particular ride, is can they really afford that car? Will the dealer be willing to sell the car at a price she is willing to pay? That's the ultimate question, the end of the journey. If the answer is yes, Dana will drive away with the car. If it is no, she will drive home in her old car, or ride the bus. The good news is that with cars, there are plenty more where that one came from. That's part of Dana's power, but more on that later. For now, the point is that everyone has their price.

The car dealership wants to sell a car. That's how they make money and they have a price that they will not go below to sell a certain car. You, on the other hand, know what you can afford and what you are willing to pay for a certain car. If these two positions meet, you will walk away with a car payment. Notice I said positions. You don't know what the final, lowest amount that the dealer is willing to sell you a particular car. And the dealer does not know the final, highest dollar you will pay for that same car. In most situations, neither of you will ever know. Sorry. The point of negotiation for BOTH sides is to try and meet at a point that is within each one of their comfort zones; low enough for the buyer, high enough to satisfy the dealer's needs.

Yet, there are many more variables to buying a car than just price. Oh, price is certainly the most important, and the yardstick which we use to brag to our friends about the great deal we negotiated. But it is not the only thing, by any means. And there is a ready supply of cars and dealerships to compete for your purchase that makes buying a car the perfect scenario to use to demonstrate the principles, or rules of negotiation.

First off, the sticker prices of new or used cars are just suggestions. My apologies to the stated policy of Saturn, who told us that they set their sticker prices low so that we didn't have to bicker over them. Hogwash on both fronts. Their stickers were not lower than their counterparts (I remember comparing) and, therefore, they had to bicker. And it didn't work, did it. You can't buy a new Saturn anymore.

In addition to price, cars come in different colors, power trains, seating, towing, luxury packages, etc. These items can be used to negotiate the final price and the final set up for a new car. Cars are also subject to outside factors like popularity (remember the ever-popular Mazda Miata that famously sold for more than the sticker price), brand identification, gas prices and dealer overhead. Lastly, don't forget that buying a car can be a very emotional purchase. It's fun. So for purposes of demonstrating the rules of negotiation, the new car buying experience has a lot to offer.

So where do you start when buying a car? In the broader sense, where does anyone start when negotiating anything? The opening salvo is the offer or demand. In the case of our Ford Edge, the opening demand is the sticker price of $41,500. This is displayed proudly on the window, along with all of the options and standard features that supposedly justify this price. You can certainly just agree to pay that price if you want, but most people don't. They know better. And trust me, the car dealers don't really expect you to pay the sticker price. If you don't believe me, just express a sincere interest in a particular vehicle on the lot, but complain that it is just more than you wanted to pay. I guarantee you the salesman will waste no time in letting you know that the sticker price is negotiable, that is before he tries to convince you that you can't live without the car. Jerry Wholesale makes it a point not to talk price at all, until he has sold the customer on how great the car they are looking at is. He believes that if Dana and Ted believe that they simply cannot live without this Ford Edge in their garage, they won't let themselves walk away without it.

For our purposes, then, the ACME's price tag of $41,500 is the opening demand. Let's step away from the Ford Edge example for a moment, though.

Absent a window sticker on a car, who should make the first move in a negotiation? Who goes first? Most people would answer that the person who wants something goes first. The seller of the car or home posts the first price, or demand. In a contract for bid, the company or agency that wants to hire out the work establishes the written specifications for the work and they let others bid how much they will perform the work for. That is probably close to what you would do if you hired a plumber. You would invite several plumbers over and tell them what you needed. They would quote you a price and you would choose the best deal for you. You might and you should negotiate further with the winner, too. If you bought a pool, you would solicit bids and try and play one off of the other to knock the price down or get the most for your money. If you are a plaintiff in a lawsuit, your attorney will ordinarily make the first move; demand settlement from the defendant who was negligent. If you are a criminal defendant, the prosecutor is likely to make the first proposal for a plea bargain, with a little nudging from your lawyer. Let's not focus on the criminal side of things.

Set aside conventional wisdom for a moment. Who goes first is really a strategy decision. There are no laws that require one side to make the first move. Just like dating; the man is traditionally charged with asking the woman out on the first date. But isn't it refreshing when the tables are turned? Sometimes. In some instances, I am not sure why we wait for the seller to make the first move, or the prosecutor, or the plaintiff.

Maybe we instinctively want someone to tell us what the price of the car is before we can analyze what we are willing to pay for it. Maybe it is as simple as the fact that we often don't know whether a person wants to sell their car or home until they tell us. There are several situations, though, where we know that the seller wants to sell his car or house. We know that a plaintiff in a civil suit is going to want money, or that the prosecutor wants some type of punishment for the crime charged. We know when a union contract comes up for renewal, we don't need the employer to tell the union how much of a raise they are or are not offering before the union knows what they want.

Since there is no rule or law requiring that either party go first, what is the advantage or disadvantage of making the first move? The biggest advantage is control. Control over the negotiation. Make no mistake about it, control is a big advantage. Maybe that's why the car dealers take the initiative and plaster their outrageous price on the window. They are not necessarily proud that they are charging tens of thousands of dollars for a hunk of metal on wheels, but if you started the bidding, they may not make as much on each sale. They are not stupid are they?

The fact is that the person who goes first sets the upper or lower parameter of the negotiation. If you want to sell your used car for $3,500 to a dealer, you need to set the price well above that level to start with. If you don't, the dealer will start low, and help control how the negotiation progresses. If you can set the first price to which you and the buyer will compare subsequent amounts, you have a better chance of manipulating what the final price will be. Going first can be a way to market your terms to the other side.

I have to confess that I unwittingly put this theory to the test during a management class in college. It was a personnel management class and the professor tried a little experiment. He broke us up into teams of two students each and paired us up against another team. Our objective was to negotiate a wage rate. One group played the role of management, the other labor. We were each given secret objectives for the discussions and we conducted our negotiations in front of the class.

I promise I was not being clairvoyant way back then, but my partner and I, who had the labor side of things, went ahead and made the first move. We were the only union pair to do so and the professor asked us after we had negotiated the best union deal of all why we decided to make the opening salvo? We told him that we wanted to have more control over where the negotiations would end up. We wanted to start out on the offensive.

Our experiment worked for the purposes of this book, not that I was thinking about writing a book in 1983; I was aggressively seeking the cheapest beer at that point, and succeeding. So was it coincidence that our team made the best deal? Yes, it probably was. Going first in a negotiation does not guarantee a better result. Sometimes it ends up being like the opening tip in a basketball game – just one little part of a game that isn't decided until the very nervous end.

Most of the time, though, I think that who goes first in a negotiation is more important than who wins the tip in a basketball game. Going first can help start you off on the offensive and help you guide the discussions in your direction. It also stirs things up when everyone expects you to wait for the other side to make a move. There is a downside, though.

When you take the initiative, you run the risk that your opening salvo will simply be too high or too low, depending on your perspective. In the real world, you may not have any idea what your potential buyer or seller, or the other side in whatever negotiation you are involved in, is thinking. You may have no clue how he or she has evaluated the subject of the discussions. If you are the buyer, you might offer more than you need to at first and send the signal that you are willing to pay more than the seller would be willing to take. The seller will simply adjust their thinking to their advantage. On the other hand, you might offer too little to begin with and send the signal that you are either playing around and are not serious or that there is simply no chance to make a sale.

The opposite is true if you are in the position of the seller. If you demand too much the first time around, the buyer may just be convinced that he or she can't afford that car or house. If you demand too little, you may inadvertently tilt the final number lower than you need to or lower than you can accept. The truth is that it does help sometimes to find out what the other side is thinking before you show your cards. Sometimes waiting for the other party to make the first move is not a bad idea.

If you do decide to go first and demand too much or offer too little, for the negotiation to actually succeed you will need to drastically change your position – and you will end up losing credibility the next time around, if there is one. Two quick points.

First, there is no substitute for knowledge and preparation. Demanding or offering too much or too little means you simply did not evaluate the item accurately. Second, everything you say or do in a negotiation means something, or should mean something. Everything you say or do has to send a signal that hopefully advances your chances of succeeding – buying that car for a good price. We will focus more on these points later. Back to the Ford Edge.

The Logic Behind the Initial Demand and Offer

How does the ACME Ford dealership set the manufacturer's sticker price for the Ford Edge? The dealer essentially buys the SUV from Ford for $X and the manufacturer, Ford Motor Company, sets a "suggested retail price" for it on the sticker. From the car company's perspective, they want to make sure that a Ford Edge has the same price in Vermont as it does in Utah, before local taxes and surcharges are added in. It makes their advertising easier, and it helps them avoid setting up competition among their exclusive dealers. It helps negotiation too; there is one basic price for everyone. This sticker price is higher than what the dealer has to pay for the car to sit on their lot, however. The infamous "dealer invoice" presumably has the price that the dealer pays for the privilege to sell the car.

So, the price of the Edge is MORE than the amount that the dealer has to sell it for in order to make a profit. The amount that the dealer can subtract from the sticker and still make a profit is likely more than simply the difference between the sticker and the invoice. But for now, Ford Motor Company sets the price higher than they know their dealers need to sell the car for because they want to give them room to negotiate. They want to give their dealers room to work with the buyer to sell more and more cars. If you are the seller, that's what you do. If you need to sell your home for $250,000, you don't put it on the market for that amount. You ask more. If you were to put it on the market for $250,000, you might wait longer for someone to buy it at that price. You give yourself some room to negotiate. You give yourself some room to go down in price, if for no other reason but to make the buyer feel as if they have made a good bargain. Same deal with lawsuits. A plaintiff attorney does not demand the amount that his client expects to receive, or the least that he or she will take, right off the bat.

The amount of leeway that a seller of a house or a used car or a seller of a business allows himself varies greatly. It varies too much and depends on the particular markets and circumstances of each individual transaction to generalize. In the case of a new car, the leeway that a dealer has is likely in the thousands, rarely the tens of thousands of dollars. In other situations, however, the opening demand may be double or more than double the eventual value of the thing bargained for.

Now that we know the initial demand for the Ford Edge, the sticker price of $41,500, what is Dana's first offer? To answer that question, Dana needs to find out a couple of things. What is a new Edge generally selling for, average, in her area? She can find this information out and this will help her determine what the value of the car is. The car or house or construction service is a commodity that has a value that varies over time, depends on the economy generally and depends on where you live. Remember the Miata – it sold for more than the initial demand for a while because that was the value that the market placed on the car. It was in high demand. So you need to determine what your local market is valuing the Edge at the time you are ready to buy it. Dana did that, remember.

After you have done that, you need to determine how much you can afford to pay for it and how much you are willing to pay for the car. Dana and Ted need to look at their own finances in detail. They need to find out how much of a down payment they can make and how much in monthly payments they can pay and still take care of Holly Terror and Bam. Kids are expensive. Kids with bad names are the worst. That is a subject of yet another book.

What they can afford depends on the market, their circumstances and their subjective analysis of what they would be willing to pay or what they can afford to pay for that vehicle. We will get into more detail about that a few chapters down the road. Two of the most important aspects of negotiating, however, start before you ever make an offer for that car.

First, you need to be prepared. Preparation means finding out what the value is in your area of whatever it is you are trying to buy. Research, internet browsing, reading up are essential. You need to be informed about that car, or house, or contractor. Secondly, you have to have a plan. You shouldn't just start negotiating with the dealer without knowing why you are offering what you are offering or without knowing where you want to end up. Ask my wife.

When we sit down with the salesman at the dealership and we start to talk money, I will not make my first offer without meeting with my wife outside the presence of the salesman. Why? We talk about what we would be willing to pay and strategize how we are going to get the salesman to meet our price. We talk about the first offer, the second offer, what we are going to say to convince the salesman he needs to go even lower and we talk about what we will accept and what we will walk away from. And we will meet and revise our strategy often as we go; adapting to whatever happens during the negotiation.

So, bring your spouse to the car dealership! Your initial offer will need to be below what you expect to pay for the car and below what your bottom line is. How much below depends on how far apart your bottom line is from the initial demand, the sticker price. Generally, if you want to buy the car for $40,000, you better offer around $38,000. Why? Because as we will see in Rule VII, you want to be in a position to split the difference at some point. If your bottom line is lower, you will need to start lower.

The same strategy is true for sellers. If someone offers you $500 for your mint condition Martin guitar and you want to sell it for $600, you should ask for at least $700. The key to the exercise (the initial demand and initial offer) is to offer an amount that you can justify as a reasonable, good faith value of the object of your affections, but an amount that leaves you room to compromise at your target price.

CHAPTER 3

THE UNSPOKEN RULES OF ETTIQUETTE

Before we get to the Eleven Rules of Negotiation, let's take a brief look at some other, unspoken but important rules. I refer to them as rules of etiquette, but this is not a chapter about bowing before the mighty Ford Corporation, or wearing a collared shirt. There are some simple rules of the game that you have a right to expect others to play by, and the other side has a right to expect you to abide by too.

The most basic rule is that no one should have to bid against themselves. If you offer $38,000 for that Ford Edge, don't offer another dime until your salesman has responded to it – has made a counter demand. If you do, you will simply be adding to your willingness to pay more for the car without consideration. Don't bid against yourself. Or maybe I should say, don't talk to yourself. That may be an easier way to explain it.

It is also a mutually understood rule, but not written in stone anywhere, that you take turns responding to each other's demands/offers. It's also part of a good salesman's mantra; make your pitch, ask for the order and then shut up. Do not say another word until your potential buyer speaks. The same is true in negotiation. You make your persuasive pitch for your offer, then let your opponent make the next move. Usually, the parties in negotiations take turns offering suggestions, offers, and counter-offers in an attempt to reach a resolution, a sale or a compromise. The Eleven Rules that follow describe what to do and what not to do during this back and forth leading up to the final offer.

Another unspoken rule is that you need to be patient. It takes time sometimes to whittle down to the final sale. By going back and forth, the parties figure out what each other will not accept and only when and if both will accept the same terms, is there an agreement, or a sale. How many different combinations of price, options, terms, conditions and services are there in a construction contract, or a union contract? How many different options come on a car? The more options or pieces, the longer it is going to take to agree on them.

So do what my wife and I do: Use the time between offers to re-group and re-evaluate our next move. Use the time to adapt. Yes, and let the other side sweat a little. That may sound mean or callous, but it can help diffuse a tense situation or help cajole the other side into coming to their bottom line (or coming to Jesus, if you prefer) that much quicker. If you appear too eager to come to a resolution, or too eager to buy that Ford Edge, you run the risk of sending the signal that you will be willing to pay whatever it takes to buy that car. The negotiation process is all about sending the right signals, after all.

As you will see in the rules that follow, you have to be willing and able to walk away from the negotiation without buying the car, or the house. If you do not think that you will be able to buy that car for your price, you have to be willing to pass. Most importantly, you have to make the salesman believe that you are perfectly willing to leave if he cannot satisfy your needs. One of the ways you convince him or her of this is through simple patience. Your calm, composed and deliberate action is your ally; use it early and often.

The other major unspoken rule can be summed in one word; integrity. The rule is that you have it. People assume that you are using it when negotiating. A lack of integrity will go a long way to ruining your attempt to buy that car, or house or settle that business deal. Integrity means that you will do what you say you will do, that you are not lying when you say something in a negotiation.

We often hear how contracts used to be agreed upon by a handshake, not with pen and paper. Legally, a handshake will still do in most circumstances. So your word needs to be your bond. If you tell the Ford salesman that you will buy that car for $37,000, you'd better be prepared to do that if he comes back and says he will agree to that. Conversely, if the salesman tells the potential customer that he will sell the Edge for $40,000 with a free undercoat, that is exactly what he better be prepared to do. Both sides need to be able to rely on each other's word alone.

I hate to bring up legalese, because this book is not about the law. But I am going to do so anyway. If a demand or an offer is made, it can be withdrawn at any time before the other side accepts it. Similarly, a counter offer is technically a rejection of the other's offer and a new demand or offer that the other side can now accept or reject, or which can be withdrawn. However, before an offer is withdrawn, the other side has a reasonable time to accept it. If he or she does so, a legally binding contract exists. Sorry. This legalese means that as soon as one side accepts the offer, the deal is done. So you cannot make an offer without being willing to abide by it.

The unwritten rule is that the demand or offer should remain open long enough to allow your buyer or seller to think about it – look more closely at the offer, talk with relatives, or clients before making a decision. That's why when you make an offer on a home, you give the buyer a day, or more, to accept it. In the case of buying a car, the same rules apply, though things generally happen much quicker. The demand or offer is deemed to remain open for a reasonable time period, or for however long the person offering says so.

When negotiating to buy that Ford Edge, the salesman might tell you that his "final price" is only good for today, or tonight; if you don't buy the car today, this price will not be available tomorrow. Certainly, someone else could always slip in and buy the car before you pull the trigger. That is always the chance you take. Your response should be – if you can stomach it – that you will not play that game. If you are uncomfortable with that time frame, kindly ask for more time. Ask the salesman for the amount of time that you need to make a decision, if the car is still available. Nine times out of ten, the salesman will agree. His time frame is his way of putting pressure on you while he still has you in the showroom. Give the salesperson the chance to give you extra time if you know you don't want to be pressured that way. If the salesman refuses, then use your leverage; walk away. Don't buy the car if you don't like the price or if you are feeling too much pressure to make a decision. Eight times out of ten, if you decide to buy the car tomorrow the price will be the same. The integrity of the salesman will not be the same, of course, but that is not your problem.

Finally, a word of caution. Once you accept the offer on the table, you have bought the farm, whatever the farm is. Legalese again. There are some situations where the law will allow you some time to renege on a deal. Generally, your verbal acceptance is enforceable in court. So is the salesman's agreement to sell the car to you on the terms agreed to. Should you get the agreement in writing? Of course you should. But just because it isn't in writing, doesn't mean that it's not valid; it is. Once the salesman agrees to the price you have offered, or you agree to his price, neither one of you can back out. So don't say "I accept" unless you mean it, and don't make an offer that you can't live with.

CHAPTER 4

RECAP BEFORE THE 11 RULES

Now you know the basics of how negotiations work. One side makes a demand, a plea designed to persuade you that $41,500 is a great price for a great SUV. Then you think about it, meet with your wife or husband, strategize and conspire. Then you respond by accepting the offer, rejecting it and walking away in disgust or laughter (not really recommended if you ever plan to return) or making a counter offer for the car. The ball is now in the salesman's court. He will likely leave you alone and pretend to talk with his sales manager. He might do so as they strategize and conspire about their next move. Then he will return and may accept your offer, reject it and complain that you are not serious so he is done negotiating (not really recommended if he wants to sell a car) or he will counter your offer.

On and on this process will continue until you buy the car, or until one of you takes their ball and walks away. My theory, such that it is, is that everyone has a range of options or scenarios that they can live with or agree to which can be placed in a circle, spatially. If you lay both circles down and they overlap, the back and forth, the give and take *should* yield a sale within the area of overlap. If your bottom line is lower than they feel they can sell you the car and make a profit or cut their loss on the car, you won't drive home in a new car. Neither of you know the other's breaking point, but usually you will end up there when all is said and done. This is the traditional, positional negotiation. Adversary negotiation, if you will.

There is that school of negotiation that advocates a more cooperative approach to negotiation; The Harvard approach. After much research on the attitudes of those negotiating, looking into the mindset of both parties as if one could know what each side is thinking and wanting, and independently determining what outcome would satisfy each side, this approach suggests being honest and up-front early on about your bottom line and working with the salesman or homeowner or businessman on the other side to mutually benefit each in the deal. This approach is backed up by their research and the science behind the parties to a negotiation. It can work and it is always a good idea to know and appreciate that the seller of that car has a legitimate need to make a profit –that's what makes this country work and what makes capitalism the greatest economic system in the world. But this cooperative approach is not the way it normally works. Forget what someone thinks *should happen*, this approach is not the way things normally happen. Why not?

Because for the Harvard approach to work, all of the parties to the negotiation have to play by these same rules. The salesman and you have to be totally honest and willing to satisfy the other. If either one of you is not willing to do so, it simply won't work. Someone will be taken advantage of and that someone will likely be the one who is trying to be cooperative. Most of the time, we do not deal with the same people when we buy a car, or a house or close a business deal. We don't follow the same family around and buy the house that they move out of every ten or so years. We don't always buy a Ford, and we don't buy a car often enough to follow the same salesman.

Trust in life and in negotiation is earned. If you are dealing with someone new, who you don't know and have never dealt with, you do so at arms length. They do the same with you. If you are buying a car from a relative, that is a different story. If you negotiate business deals with the same company often, or with the same attorney about the same type of cases, trust is earned, built up and the negotiations can and often do become more cooperative, and less adversarial. After a while, you both know how the other is likely to evaluate the deal and it is easier to determine whether you can come to an agreement.

For the rest of us, and for the vast majority of negotiations in life, we proceed with caution because we don't know if we can trust that the other side will be cooperative even if we are. I don't think that is a bad thing, I think it is simply reality.

So what comes next? The rest of the negotiations are filled with each side trying to bring the other side within their circle, within the terms that they want or are willing to accept. You will try and persuade the salesman that the car is not worth that sticker price and convince him to sell it to you at a price you are comfortable with. The salesman will try and convince you that the SUV is a great buy at his price. How you try and convince the salesman to lower his price is up to you. Let's start going through the 11 rules that, if followed, can help give you the best chance to be successful.

CHAPTER 5

RULE NUMBER I, BE REALISTIC

OK, if you can't follow Rule Number One, the other rules will not likely work. The absolute best way to give yourself the best chance of buying your car at your price is to accurately assess the value of the car. The absolute best thing that the seller can do to give himself or herself the best chance of selling a car is to accurately assess the value of the car. The absolute best way that a litigator can settle his case for his client is to accurately assess the value of the claim. The absolute best way for the sellers of a home to sell their home is to accurately evaluate it –price it right. See a pattern?

It sounds so simple, too simple really, but it in any negotiation you need to put a value on the object you are trying to buy or sell. I have negotiated many lawsuits on behalf of a variety of clients, and the most important factor in successfully resolving the cases was not my skills as a negotiator. The biggest factor that determined success was whether my client and I had accurately determined the value of the case, and whether the other side had done the same. I couldn't control whether the other side was realistic about their case. You can't control whether the Ford salesman will be realistic about his coveted product either, or whether the owner of that home you want to buy will be able to detach their pride from the reality of the market. But you can control whether you evaluate the Ford Edge accurately.

I did this many years ago, again by coincidence, and proved my own point. Fresh out of college with a business degree that netted me a job making $12,500 per **year**, I needed to buy a car. My old Ford Maverick, a great car, just did not fit the bill for an up and coming businessman with a salary. Admittedly, $12,500 a year was not a big salary even in 1984, but I did not want to admit that at the time. So I found a beautiful new Ford Thunderbird. I should say right now that I do not have any particular fondness for Fords, though I did own that great Maverick and later owned a Mustang that was nothing but trouble.

I brought my dad with me to help me negotiate the deal. My dad could have written this book. He remains the best negotiator of cars that I have ever run across, mainly I think, because he has an intrinsic sense of what a car is worth and of what is a good deal and what is a bad one. Long story shorter, he and I negotiated a really good deal on a beautiful, new blue Thunderbird that I really wanted. We could not have negotiated a better price for that car. There was a three day period in which I could back out of the deal.

That evening, probably at the request of my dad, I went over my income, rent, food, entertainment (I was boring, not much there), utilities, and miscellaneous expenses in great detail at the kitchen table. I determined, on my own, that I could not afford the cost of the new car I had just purchased. It wasn't too late to make this determination since I had a period of time in which to get out of the deal, and I did just that. Then I bought a used Mustang that I could afford.

The lesson is that if you can only afford a car that costs $25,000, don't try and negotiate to buy a Ford Edge that is valued at $38,000 or $40,000. You might be able to make a great deal, but that doesn't help you if you can't really afford it. On the other hand, don't walk into the Ford dealership with so much confidence in your negotiating skills that you convince yourself that you can negotiate the price of that $41,000 SUV down to $25,000 or $30,000; it won't happen.

The same is true for the other foot. The salesman who believes that he can sell every SUV that is selling on the market for $40,000 or a little less than $41,000, will not make many sales. The homeowner who is convinced that his dream home for the last ten years is worth $250,000, when every real estate agent he meets tells him that it is worth $200,000 at the very most, has a big problem. The problem for both is that they have not realistically valued what they want to sell.

In theory, that new car, or home or the value of the business's services has only one objective value, or a range within which others are going to be willing to pay for it. That value is whatever someone else is willing to pay, for sure, but that range can be determined. How would you go about determining what the value of a new Ford Edge SUV is in a particular market?

Every negotiator is bound by the market. No matter how good a negotiator is, they can't avoid the market. Each Ford Edge, each lawsuit, every new home has a value. Every man has a price, the saying goes. We have talked about setting your goals, trying to determine what it is you want in your Ford and what you are willing or able to pay for it. Now you need to look objectively at what the Ford's value is – what the seller may need in order to sell it to you. You are not going to know for sure, ever probably. But the better you are able to assess how much the seller is going to be willing to take, the better off you will be.

Of course, there is always the age-old question; what did the seller pay for the car? What is his cost? The seller has to be able to make a profit on each car, most of the time, so the price of the car will usually be the absolute lowest value that the dealer can sell the car for, but more likely the dealer's bottom line is going to be his cost plus a little more.

Some dealers purchase their cars from Ford using a floor plan. This simply means that they borrow money from a bank to buy the cars from Ford. When they do this, they pay the bank interest on the loan. Thus, each month or week that an Edge sits on a dealer's lot, the interest payments pile up. The longer that a car has sat on the dealer's lot, the more it costs the dealer and the less he will be willing to sell it for. So look for the lonely Edge at the back of the lot that has been there for a while.

Sometimes Ford will provide incentives for the dealers to sell cars. If they sell so many cars in a month, or a year, Ford may pay the dealer. Maybe the dealer gets a kickback if they sell so many Ford Edges. In either event, every car they sell has a value that Ford provides to them. So, with the floor plan and dealer incentives, they may sell one Ford Edge for less than what it appears they paid for it.

Quite simply, the more information that you have about the car and the dealer and the dealers in your area, the easier it will be for you to determine the value of the car. Knowledge is strength. I have negotiated several civil lawsuits for clients, plaintiffs and defendants, and my ability to accurately assess (or more accurately, my ability to evaluate) the value of the damages claim was the biggest determinant of whether I was able to successfully negotiate the case. In order to evaluate how much that Ford is worth to the dealer, you need to know what you want and can afford, you need to know what the market will bear and you need to know what the dealer is likely to accept.

I said likely to accept. That is because you will not be able to assess everything. You will have to guess a little. You can look on websites for the average price of a particular vehicle in your geographic area. You can find some indications about what the dealer invoices are. You can probably search websites and determine if the dealer owns or rents their lot; some will advertise the former. The dealer may show you the invoice. But you are not going to know everything. The more you know, the more strength you have in the negotiation. But you are probably reading this and thinking that the dealer has most of the strength, because they know all the costs, incentives, reasons to go below or above their invoice price and they know that if they negotiate a good deal with you, they may be able to sell the next car a little cheaper than that to make the sale. All that is true, but don't give up just yet. What leverage, or power do you have?

Well, you have the amount of cash that you are able to use as a down payment on the car. The more cash you put down, the easier it is for the dealer to finance the sale. People with bad credit that the dealer has to shop around in order to find a loan, costs them time and money. If they have to get a loan for you at a higher risk lender, not only are your payments likely to be more, but the dealer may have to pay more to the lender for the deal. If you can decrease their costs and risks, you are a more favored customer.

There are websites which track the average selling prices of new cars. Does this mean that whatever the website says is the lowest you will be able to buy the car for is correct? No. It gives you an idea about how much of a discount you could reasonably expect at that time in your area, that's all. What price you will be able to buy a particular SUV depends on a lot of other factors. The price of gas and whether gas prices are on the way up or down will matter. Whether the Edge is a particularly popular brand in your area, or whether SUVs in general are. The actual cost of the car to the dealer, including their infamous invoice price, but also whether they receive any incentives from Ford for selling an SUV, or certain number of cars per year, month or other time period and how close they are to that goal when you walk into the showroom, are all factors that will influence the dealer's bottom line.

The dealer's price may also depend on how much their overhead is for their business. If they are carrying a high overhead, that may limit their ability to deal. On the other hand, if they have purchased their cars on a floor plan, meaning that they have borrowed money to buy the cars from Ford to put on their lot, they may be willing to take less on an SUV that has been sitting on their lot for a long time; so they can cut off their interest payment on that car.

The amount of cash that you are willing to put down as a down payment may help you shave off some money from the price of the car. Maybe you have a car to offer in trade. That may help you reduce the price of that new Ford Edge, but you will need to do your homework on the value of your trade-in. This book is not about how to value a used car, but it is worth noting that the value of a used car to a new car dealer is NOT equal to its retail value to a direct purchaser. Translation? You will almost always be able to get more money for your old car if you sell it direct rather than trade it in. I do not recommend negotiating for the purchase of the new car and then when you think that the dealer is at its lowest figure, throwing in the fact that you have a trade. That sounds really good in theory, but it goes against one of the earlier, unwritten rules – integrity. I don't think springing a trade-in on a salesman at the last minute will help the negotiations, I think it will be more likely to sink them. You can talk about the price of the new car, separate from their offer on your trade-in, but being up-front about your intention to trade in your old car is the way to go.

You also have the power of your feet. This will be covered later, but perhaps the biggest power you have is the fact that when buying a car, there is no shortage of comparable vehicles available at dealers hungry for your business. Most sales persons are taught that statistically, if a person leaves the store without purchasing a car (or a stereo, or a coat) the likelihood that they will come back later and make the sale decreases greatly. They need to keep you there as long as they can, ogling at the car they want you to buy. Once you leave, they know their chances of making a sale virtually disappear.

When buying that Ford Edge, you also have the power of numbers. That is, the numbers of other dealers out there anxious to try and sell you the same SUV. Find out what other Edges are on other dealers' lots. Bring newspaper advertisements for Ford Edges and the big discounts that other dealers are willing to make. Talk with other dealers and negotiate with them to see what price they will quote you so you can use this information when trying to negotiate with a subsequent dealer.

It pays to shop around, and it pays to be willing to shop around some more.

Probably the most power you have, though, is the amount of information that you have been able to accumulate about the car, the dealer, the market; all of the things we have been talking about. Knowledge is strength, and the more knowledge you can get, the more power you will have. This is true in any negotiation. Buying the Ford Edge is just the example I use, but being able gather information about the subject of the negotiation is just as important when buying a house or bidding on a construction contract.

Whether you are buying a car or settling a lawsuit, information about your own situation and that of the seller, or your opponent, is crucial. It's also time consuming and could be painful. You might find out that you cannot afford that Ford Edge after all. Or you might find out that your client's case is not as strong as you thought it was. Regardless, you need to know your own position and the position of the other side before you sit down with the dealer.

The bottom line is that you have to be able to realistically value the price of that new Ford Edge. And you have to be willing and able to pay that amount. If that is too much for you, find another new car whose value fits your ability to pay for it. I did that when I abandoned my dream of a new Thunderbird, eventually.

CHAPTER 6

RULE NUMBER II, SET A GOAL

What is the best case scenario for the purchase of your car; what car with which options would you really like to buy? What is your goal in your negotiation? What do Dana and Ted really want on their new car? This sounds like it should be the first rule, doesn't it? It could be I guess, but I think that you need to know what the value of that SUV is to find out whether you can afford it before you sit down to set specific goals. Someone once said that the biggest reason plans fail is that people fail to plan. That sounded good and many people, myself included, have often repeated it. And it is especially true for negotiation because I don't think a lot of people really think about where they want to end up in a negotiation nor do they think about what steps they need to take to get there. In negotiation as in life, preparation really is the key.

Another reason I chose setting a goal as the second most important rule as opposed to the first is that anyone can set a goal. You can set a goal of buying a new Cadillac Escalade for $20,000, and dream about offering the dealer the sum of $10,000 to start with, slowly inching up to $20,000 when you say that is the most you will pay, or else you walk out that door! In your dream, your methodical and slow walk up to offering $20,000 and your bold take it or leave it approach, threatening to walk out that showroom door, wins the day. Forget what an Escalade is worth, your mastery of *Smoke Signals* has allowed you to reach your goal. That is really a dream. A dream that will not possibly come true, unless you are negotiating to buy that Escalade that was nearly totaled by a recent Hurricane.

Any fool can set a goal. But if you have a prayer of buying that Ford Edge, your goal better be a realistic one. In fact, you can make too much of a goal. If it becomes the sole yardstick by which you judge whether you have made a good deal, you may be sorely disappointed because the best deal you can make for that car may be a little different than your goal, even if you have been realistic in evaluating its value. So what is the purpose of making a goal in the first place? It is so you can determine your strategy. That's it. That's all it is.

Your goal is where you would like to end up. In the context of buying the Ford Edge, Dana and Ted's goal is to buy the car with the options they want at the price they want to afford and can afford. They have researched the approximate prices that Fords are selling for in their area, they know what options they need and they know what they are hoping to pay for it. Their goal is not just money, of course.

Sometimes we think of money as being the only aspect of a negotiation. It's not. It is only one factor to consider when buying a car; only one part of your goal. So you need to determine what options you want on your car and what options you can't do without. Everything needs to be considered and prioritized. Seating, engine size, sun-roof, tilt control, fancy stereo system, GPS, heated seats, four wheel drive, extra seating, do you need to tow a trailer are all things you may really need on your Ford. Prioritize.

Your goals are not necessarily what you have to have in the car, they are what you want. Best case scenario. But by prioritizing, you try to determine what is the most important to you in a car and what is the least – the absolutely necessary to the expendable. Almost everything is, or should be negotiable. But there are trade offs. Certain options on the SUV may be expendable if replaced by others. Maybe you can do without an SUV with a sun-roof if you can get a better price or a certain color. It's probably impossible to anticipate all of the different combinations of options that you might accept in an SUV at a certain price. It likely will depend on what is on the lot. In any event, it is important to think about all of the options that you want in your car and prioritize them.

All of the rest of the rules in this book are designed to lead to one result; you buying the car that you want at a price you like and can afford. Meeting your goals is the game. So, you have to know what it is you want before you can begin negotiating to get it. You also have to presume that the other side is doing the same thing. Like that evil insurance company that is hiring their team of lawyers to defeat your claim, the car dealers are constantly determining how much their cars cost them, how much it is costing them to keep each car on the lot another day, what the demand is for their cars, which cars are likely to sell fast, which aren't, and they have a very good idea of what they want to sell each car on their lot for. They know their goals.

This doesn't just apply to buying a car, or a house. Any seasoned negotiator has an idea of where they want to end up. Countries send teams of negotiators to work out treaties or reduce military weapons. There may not have been a price tag or a sticker price for concluding the SALT talks of the 1970s with Russia (I am showing my age here), but there were plenty of options that both sides bargained for. Both sides had goals for the talks, concessions that they wanted to wrest from the other side. Each had to begin by knowing exactly what they were willing to give up before they sat down to the table. Buying the Ford Edge is not any different, but it is less explosive.

CHAPTER 7

RULE NUMBER III, WHAT IS YOUR BOTTOM LINE

One plus two equals three. Rule I plus Rule II equals Rule III. You have determined your goals for buying the Ford Edge. You know what you want on the car and what you can afford. You know all about the market for the Edge in your area and have done your research on the dealer or dealers in your area. Now you need to put that value on the end result. You need to know your bottom line – or close to it. In our example, Dana and Ted need to have a heart to heart to figure out when to walk away and when to run.

Setting a goal in Rule Number II was designed to let you, and Dana and Ted, know what it was you wanted; the best case scenario as it were. That is true in any negotiation. They need to have an idea of what they want to accomplish. The information in Rules Number I and II should have been their assessment of what that Edge could realistically be bought for, or how much that home or lawsuit is worth.

Admittedly, Rules I and II were basic; perhaps overly simple. It doesn't take an expert to suggest that you need to go on a fact finding mission before trying to negotiate with a dealer to buy a car. It's not earth shaking advise that you sit down and find out what it is you want in a car, or a home for that matter, before you look for one. Yet, I don't think most people really plan for a negotiation, they just show up and one breaks out. But the salesmen plan. They train for it. Jerry Wholesale thinks about it every day, constantly. You need to do a little work planning for it, too, don't you think?

If you don't do the research or planning, you won't be able to accurately put your value on the Ford Edge, or on that house you want to buy. The more inaccurate you are in your assessment, the less chance you have of buying a Ford Edge at a good deal. This rule, Number III, is the basis for the rest of your negotiation and for the rest of the rules. Rule III is simply figuring out your bottom line.

The sellers or the new car dealers do the same thing. Jerry Wholesale's bosses have determined how much money they need for that Ford Edge on their lot in order to make a profit and continue their business. Dana and Ted need to find out how much they are willing to pay for their car based on what they have learned and what they want in the car. They won't know what the dealer's bottom line is, and Jerry Wholesale won't know what Dana's and Ted's is, so they're even; kind of.

As I said in the last chapter, the ability of the buyer and seller to accurately value the car, or assess their bottom lines, is really the biggest determinant of whether a sale occurs. And it is not just your assessment. If the dealer has an inflated sense of what the market will bear, what people are going to be willing to pay for that Edge, they will set their bottom line too high and they won't make the sale. Jerry might get the boot! If Dana and Ted value the car too low or over-estimate their negotiating skill, they won't buy the car either.

Usually, both sides have a range of prices and options that they will accept in a sale. Think of these ranges of options that the buyer and seller have as circles. If the circles don't overlap at all, the negotiation simply won't succeed, unless someone throws in their towel. If they do overlap, a deal is possible.

So why wouldn't these circles intersect, or these ranges overlap? There are two basic reasons.

First, if it is simply not possible to resolve the issue. If you walk into the Ford dealer with a bottom line of $25,000 (no trade-in to offer) to buy a Ford Edge that sells for $41,0000, you are likely well below the bottom line of any seller in your area. You have undervalued the car horribly and are doomed to fail.

Second is the other side of that coin. If the dealer has decided that it needs to make an inordinately high profit on that Edge, much above the going price for an Edge in their area, chances are the dealer won't make the sale.

Both of these scenarios are usually the result of one side having un-realistic expectations. The seller may have an unrealistic belief that their car is somehow special and worth more than it really is. On the other hand, the buyer might have an un-realistic belief that the car can be bought for less than its actual value. In the case of a new car, that may be the result of listening to others brag about their great deal. Fortunately or unfortunately, car dealers are usually not guilty of being un-realistic, but they are good at negotiating a better than market price for their cars.

Maybe there is at least a third reason sales don't happen that I just have to mention. There will be a chapter later on this too. That third reason is personal. The personalities, emotions or sensitivities of the negotiators sometimes get in the way. Jerry Wholesale has to be careful he does not offend his potential customer. Any seller has to be careful how they try and persuade a potential customer. For example, when Dana tells Jerry that she would like to see that V6 Ford Edge on the lot, Jerry probably should refrain from telling her that as a woman, she doesn't need six cylinders. Not even Ted will be able to restrain the rage within her after a sexist comment, and no matter what offer Jerry will make, I would bet that it won't be good enough to get the deal done. Dana and Ted will march into another dealer who won't insult them and buy a Ford Edge for the same price.

Sometimes we let our egos, or our sensitivities get the better of us. Sometimes we say the wrong thing, or lose our temper and the negotiations take a turn for the worse. When that happens, it may not matter that your circles intersect; the negotiation will fail because of injury. There may be a referee to throw a flag and restore order – Ted might calm Dana down, or say something equally insulting to Jerry that brings a smile to his wife's face; the manager may step in and save Jerry, or Jerry will make Dana and Ted an offer they can't refuse. A lot of times, however, there is no intervening act to save the deal. OK, back to the bottom line.

For the buyer, you have to determine at what price you are likely to be able to buy that Ford Edge given the options you want and the market for the car in your area. While your goal might be to buy that car with every desired option for one price (best case scenario), your research may show that the actual value of the car is more, or your price will not buy you all of those options. That is why we talked about prioritizing the list of options on the car, the options that you want, and those you really, really want or need. That is why most everything should be considered negotiable.

It doesn't sound logical to say that your goal is not your bottom line. But if you are going to be able to buy that car or that home or sell your home, your bottom line has to be accurate. You can negotiate to fully meet your goal, buy that car at your price with all the bells and whistles you want, but your bottom line is different. The dealer would love to sell you that car for the sticker price, and he will gladly do so for you if you ever want to ask. But the dealer's bottom line is quite different. It has to be.

In my litigation experience, most of the time my evaluations of claims were dead-on. I am not bragging. One of the reasons I was able to be successful is that my opponent did the same thing; accurately evaluated his or her case and our evaluations overlapped. We were both realistic, accurate. If the case couldn't be settled, it wasn't because I hadn't done my homework. I also recall one case I negotiated for an injured person where the settlement exceeded our realistic expectations.

And that is the lesson of the interplay between your goal and your bottom line. Don't be afraid to negotiate for you goal, but remember that most of the time you are going to be able to buy that car for its reasonable value in the market at the time you are negotiating. That should be your bottom line.

CHAPTER 8

RULE NUMBER IV, YOUR COMPOSURE; KEEP IT

This rule is the easiest to explain but undoubtedly the most difficult to keep. I will wager that if you negotiate often enough, you will violate this rule at least once. As soon as you do, you will instinctively know that you made a mistake. But here is the rule, nonetheless.

Keep you composure. Negotiating is nothing more than persuading someone else to agree with you. You need to convince the other person that your solution is right. There are so many ways to do this, and the next seven rules and the remainder of this book will suggest different approaches. Losing your temper, though, is not among these tactics. It simply won't work.

That is not to say that you should never show disappointment or anger. Sometimes a little righteous indignation sends a strong signal. There is a difference between righteous indignation and a violent reaction or a swearing match. There is a difference between being outraged and personalizing your adversary.

I have lost my temper and violated this rule. The first inevitable result of any outburst is that whatever you were discussing is over. If your opponent is smart and thinking logically, he or she will not take the bait and respond to you in kind. He or she will simply walk away. The negotiation will not continue until the offender has apologized or the situation has calmed down.

The second inevitable result of an outburst is that the offender will no longer be in control of the situation. Having to apologize does not put a person in a position of strength.

The next move after the apology is up to the other person who is now in a position to be magnanimous and move the talks in his direction. If the other person is thinking clearly and has read this book, he will take the opportunity you have handed him to graciously accept your humble mea culpa and take control of the rest of the negotiation. The aggressor will become the reactor. The offender of this Rule Number IV will instantly be relegated to playing defense.

One of the themes of this book is the notion that you need to give yourself the best chance to negotiate a deal that meets your goals, or falls within your bottom line. Losing your temper is counter-productive at best; it can be a total deal breaker at worst.

In the last chapter, I mentioned Jerry insulting (I think the verb is "dissing" in today's vernacular) Dana by telling her that as a woman, she did not need a V6 Ford Edge. Jerry Wholesale would be equally guilty of telling a man that he should not buy a van since it isn't manly enough; look at that cool Mustang convertible in the showroom instead. We all say things that either are insulting without meaning to be, or don't take into consideration that there are reasons why people want to buy the car they have chosen; or the house they are bidding on. When negotiations take a personally insulting turn, bad things happen. Not only do negotiators need to keep their temper, they have to be very careful that they don't personalize or insult, or bruise the ego of their opponent. We may think we don't have an ego, we aren't easily offended, but we all have our limits. Often, we aren't as thick skinned as we think; neither are your opponents in a negotiation. What's worse, when we negotiate with a stranger we have no way of knowing whether he or she is thick or thin skinned, or what might not float their boat.

Yet, it will happen to you. You will lose your temper, or say something wrong; Dana will personally insult Jerry or vice versa. Your adversary may lose his temper when negotiating with you, too. That puts you in the driver's seat, so don't despair. There are at least two ways to approach the negotiation after someone – meaning you - loses his or her composure.

The offender could directly offer his sincere apology for the incident, for overreacting to the situation; a gracious gesture to immediately diffuse the situation. After Jerry gauges that Dana is not a four-cylinder girl, he could immediately feign jocularity; "I was just kidding. Lots of women who look like you have lead feet and need more horses under the hood – right Ted?" Or, "wow, I did not know you were the racy type. Maybe I could interest you in that little pony convertible with the Mach I drivetrain over there while we leave Ted with the mini-vans." Needless to say, Jerry needs a new diffuser. Either one of these responses would only make things worse. But he could simply apologize and let Dana know that he has some six cylinders on the lot she might be interested in.

But, there is no question that if Jerry is to continue negotiations or if you will continue to have to deal with the same individual in other situations, you and he will have to mend the fences directly. You will have to do a better job at apologizing than Jerry. And if you have lost your temper, you need to be the one who extends the olive branch.

The problem is that an immediate apology might put you in a severe and distinct disadvantage. Even Ted would know that Jerry is now at the mercy of Dana after his insensitivity. Ted may know that better than anyone, but that is a story for another book. The truth is that if your negotiations are not over, you are going to be putting yourself in a subordinate position. As we said before, you will be playing defense right away. Your adversary will try and use your need to apologize as a need for you to capitulate further in the negotiations. This is not a position that you want to be in, of course.

While there is no question that the offender (Jerry and you) will need to return the relationship to a more cordial, professional one, sometimes an immediate apology creates an immediate disadvantage.

The second approach is to act as if nothing happened and initiate the next conversation in the negotiations. Calmly continue your discussions using the same professional and cordial manner that you should have maintained all along. The offender (Jerry and you) should affirmatively take to the offense and start the negotiations again. Jerry might immediately determine what V6 Ford Edge's he has on the lot and take Dana and Ted over to see them, without delay. Maybe he grabs a key and a license plate so they can take a little test drive. What does this do?

First, it helps Jerry regain control of the discussion without the baggage of an immediate apology. It tells Dana and Ted that he is moving on. Without an awkward apology that is likely to seem insincere and may be even more insulting (see above), Jerry is telling Dana silently that he is OK with the six-cylinder thing and is more than willing to show her a car she is interested in. Moving on without the immediate mea culpa tells your adversary that you are so comfortable with your idea that you refuse to miss a beat.

This approach is not easy. Your first reaction is to not say a word and wait for the other person to say something (pray that he does?) or to quickly apologize to diffuse the situation you created. Waiting for the other person to make the first move, however, will only ensure that the other person will be able to take control of the negotiations. If you want to buy that car, or home or continue to work to successfully conclude the negotiation, you are best served by taking the initiative and trying to not put yourself on the defensive.

This approach requires you to resist the temptation to break down and beg for forgiveness. We all know that personalizing a negotiation or losing ones temper is a mistake. But you don't have to make things worse for yourself by actively allowing the other side to take full advantage of your violation of this rule. You really don't have to apologize and talk your way out of every bad situation you put yourself in. After you have bought that car, after the negotiations are either successful or not, you will have plenty of time to apologize – as you must – to regain your self-respect. This strategy sounds hardcore at first, but remember that losing your temper is inevitable sometimes; it is a learning experience. Your adversary will likely either have lost his temper in the past or come close to having done so with you. The tension can and will pass. You do need to be the one to be gracious but you don't need to allow your grace to put you at a greater disadvantage.

When I lost my composure I felt bad and embarrassed. I wanted to immediately bring things back to where they had been before my outburst. But once the genie is out of the bottle, you can't just shove it back in. When it happens to me, I continue the negotiations, as if nothing had happened. I do sincerely apologize after our deal is done. And I live to negotiate again. I never discuss it again. I learn my lesson and move on. So will you.

The same is true when things get personal. If you are following this rule to the T, you don't personalize the negotiation. Not because you may not have strong feelings about your house, car or the work that you do; we all do. You follow this rule because to put yourself in the best position to buy that car or that house, or negotiate that contract for your business, you can't make the exercise personal. Put on your thick skin and remember that words have meaning; all of them do in a negotiation. And words have the ability to influence the actions of the other side. More on words later. If things get personal and you are the offender, you will need to set the record straight; sooner or later. Rule number IV, don't put yourself in that position. Let your opponent be the one who gets personal.

SUVs are popular now. The Ford Edge is a smart choice, but you can use these rules to buy whatever car or truck you like.

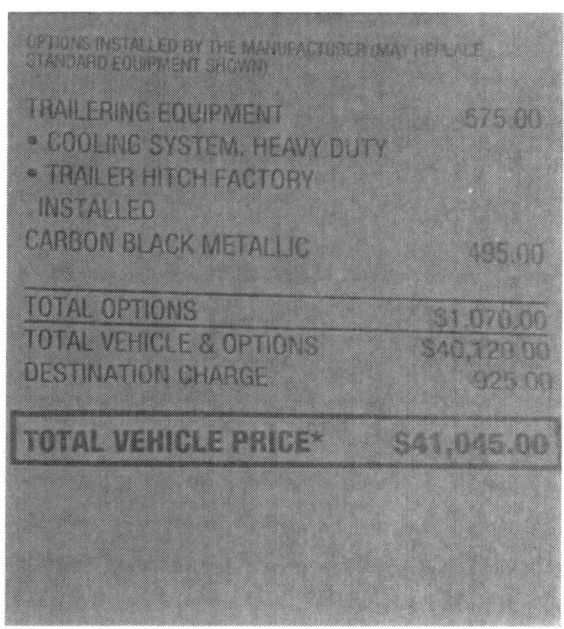

The Suggested Retail Price is just a suggestion. It is only the opening offer.

Home sweet home. For the right price, of course.

A contract is legally binding, the terms are negotiable.

CHAPTER 9

RULE NUMBER V, BE ABLE TO READ THE SMOKE SIGNALS FROM THE OTHER SIDE

One of the most difficult, but important, things to do is to find out where the other side needs to end up in the negotiations. Theoretically, the other side in any negotiation has done exactly what you have done, if they have read this book. They have determined what it is that they can accept. If what they can accept, their circle within which they will agree, intersects with your circle you should, in theory, be successful. In theory you should be able to buy that car, sell that house or win that contract.

The trouble is that you know what you want, but you don't know what your opponent wants. In fact, you may never know for sure what their bottom line is. If you agree to buy that car, do you immediately tell your salesman that you would have been willing to pay one thousand dollars more? That would be the honest thing to do. It would help that salesman figure out what people might be willing to pay in the future. But you don't do it. Nobody does. The salesman will NOT tell you what he would have been willing to sell you that car for. If you have actually done this, shame on you. Don't ever do that again (see the chapter on Saving Face later).

After the deal is done, those matters are irrelevant. In serious poker games, a person who was bluffing doesn't announce it after he or she rakes in your money. This information would only poison the well for any future relationship between you and seriously hamper that person's bluff in the future. But in the middle of your discussions, knowing where your opponent needs to be would be priceless. The good news is that you can determine what the other side is thinking indirectly; by listening very, very carefully.

Let's look at that Ford Edge the Meriweather's want to buy. Right off the bat, Jerry Wholesale shows the Meriweather's his starting point, the sticker price. He may do so proudly, if he thinks Ted is ready to pay full price. Or he may do so sheepishly, letting Dana know that everything is negotiable; after all, this is Jerry Wholesale she is talking to, Mr. Sale. In either event, the sticker is the dealer's first demand that Dana pay them $41,500 for that particular car with its laundry list of options. What does this initial demand say about the dealer's bottom line?

Well, if we know that the market for this particular car is weak (gas prices are increasing, this is last years model and the last of the old body style), then the car may be bought for at or below the amount of the general markup for the car. If the markup for this car is usually 12%, maybe this car could be bought for around $35,000. If the car you are looking at had a sticker price of $150,000 (your new Bentley or Rolls), maybe the car could be bought for around $132,000.

The question is, what is the ordinary dealer markup for this make and model? What is the profit margin? The dealer should not be expected to sell the car at a loss, they are in the business to make money not lose it. Jerry will reiterate this to several people over the course of a week. There are other factors that will affect how low the dealer COULD go (whether the dealer is willing to do so is another question): Does the dealer have a floor plan, ie does it buy its inventory on credit? What are the bonuses or incentives from the manufacturer for the sale of that Ford Edge? Many of these questions will not be knowable or readily apparent, so how do you go about determining what the dealer's bottom line is? How should Dana and Ted figure out what the dealer's bottom line is?

They need to listen to the salesman. Listen to what Jerry says, no matter how painful or difficult that might be. Take him by his word; it's all anyone can do. Listen to the words and phrases that Jerry uses as he tries to convince Ted and Dana that his next demand is reasonable. Pay attention to what Jerry is telling Dana about the virtues of the options the car has – leather seats, engine size, sunroof, back seat TV, six way power seats for driver and passenger. These items add to the price. If Dana is willing to do without them, she might be able to buy a Ford Edge at her price if she starts subtracting these options at the end.

But the most important thing to remember about the negotiation is that the salesman should be sending you signals about the price that he or she will accept. Most people who negotiate regularly, as salesmen surely do, choose their words carefully. Jerry may sound like he is one big bag of hot air, happy to listen to his own words of wisdom. But if he is any kind of a salesman, he is carefully choosing his babble. If you are not careful while listening to him, you could miss an important signal. No, the salesman is not going to wave a car key in front of you and tell you that you are getting sleepy, very very sleepy, and you need to buy this car for $40,000. But he or she is going to drop hints as they go.

If Jerry sits down with faux exhaustion and says, "We can't get to where you are", that probably seems to Dana and Ted like an innocuous statement, almost pessimistic. Yet, this preface tells you something. Jerry is telling Dana (and Ted, if he is listening) that his next demand will not meet their offer, but it also tells Dana (let's forget about Ted, until it is time to wake him up to leave) that whatever he comes back with is not his last move. He wants to keep going, but he is telling Dana that she needs to increase her offer, too.

What if Mr. Jerry Wholesale comes back to Dana and tells her, "I might be able to do $38,000, but I certainly can't sell you this car for what you are offering." This is not an a-typical statement by a car salesman in the middle of negotiations. And it should tell Dana at least two very important things. Jerry is not just shooting the bull. First off, if Jerry tells Dana that he might be able to sell that car for $38,000, this means that he would most certainly agree to sell her that car for $38,0000, and probably can do even better. Why? Because as will be pointed out later in this book, a negotiator should NEVER EVER mention a price that the negotiator would not agree to. Don't pay attention to the word "might", pay attention to the dollar figure. Regardless of the official price that the salesman is touting, if the salesman mentions a lower number in conversation, that is the new unofficial demand. Jerry will deny it when out on the social circuit, if he has one, but he knows he can't mention a number to Dana that he could not accept.

This type of statement is also telling Dana that she needs to increase her offer to buy the car. How much? Well, $38,000 will do it, but if a salesman is going to tell you definitively that he can't sell the car at your price, he is sending you a signal that your price is not in the ballpark. You either need to get in the ballpark near $38,000, or maybe you should be talking about another car.

That is the second signal that the salesman is telling you when he says that "I certainly can't sell you this car for what you are offering". The unspoken, inferred message is that there may be another car that he could sell you for close to your price. If your price is at or near the most you wanted to pay for that car, this may be a very important signal. He is telling you he won't sell you that particular Ford Edge for your price. But there may be a car on his lot that he needs to get rid of, that has a few less luxury options, or that he has more room to negotiate price. Maybe he has a car that has been on the lot too long, eating up interest payments on the loan they took out to buy it. Maybe it is a currently unpopular color. For whatever reason, the salesman may have suggested that he has an alternative option.

Every price or dollar figure that the salesman mentions is a signal all its own. A good, honest salesman will not mention any price that he is unwilling to accept, period. If a salesman tells you that he might be able to sell you that Ford Edge for

$38,000, and later says he couldn't do it after you agree to pay it, walk away. This is true if you are negotiating to buy a boat, house, contract for construction or services, etc. Part of the art of sending signals to the other side is to make sure that whatever amount that you mention at any time, is an amount you could live with – no exceptions. The other side needs to be able to trust that when you suggest that you could pay a certain amount, you will do so. You are entitled to the same trust. So when buying that Ford Edge, listen to any sales price that the salesman throws out there. He is sending you a message that that price is agreeable. Most of the time, that price will not be their bottom line either.

It's not just the price that you need to listen to, but listen for signals from the salesman about other things. When Jerry starts talking about all of the options that this Ford Edge has and how this justifies the demand he is making, he is trying to justify his price and persuade Dana to pay more. When he is talking to Dana about the financing options that are available and how she and Ted could qualify for a low rate, or spread payments out over a longer period of time, he is trying to shift her focus from the bottom line cost of the car. He is trying to make his price more palatable. If the Jerry does not tell Dana that "$X" is his bottom line, the lowest he can go, then he is telling her that he might be able to sell that car for less. We will talk later about how you send signals back, but when Jerry talks about all the options on the car, Dana needs to send the signal that she and Ted know the options as compared with other cars or other dealers, or ads in the newspaper. They have taken these options into account when they evaluated their price. If Dana and Ted are more interested in the monthly payments than the bottom line, then Jerry has given them an opportunity to work on lowering the monthly payments to meet their needs. If they are less concerned with the financing aspects but more concerned with the bottom line, then Dana needs to re-direct the conversation back to the bottom line and not allow herself to be distracted. In both of these cases, Jerry is clearly not done negotiating and has further to go before he is at his bottom line. Dana should let Jerry talk, then talk back with him. Jerry is sending the signal that he believes that a sale can be made and he wants to keep talking.

On the other hand, if Dana and Ted are more concerned with other aspects of the deal, other than price, they also need to listen to what he is saying about what is important to them. Maybe they are interested in different financing options (the price is not a problem at this point), or they really have to have a package of engine options that will allow she and Ted to tow that big camper trailer or boat up a hill. Maybe the price is fine, but they need more bells and whistles on the particular car they are talking about and Jerry could add these options in if they were so inclined. We will talk endlessly in this book about price, the bottom line for purposes of the Meriweathers and their quest to buy the Ford Edge. But the same rules apply no matter what term is being negotiated. You and Dana (and Ted too, if he can keep his eyes off of the Ford Edge they want to buy) need to listen to the salesman. Listen to how he says things, but maybe more importantly, listen to what he is saying. Most of the time, when the salesperson, Jerry Wholesale, comes back and sits down he will NOT have a happy face.

"Whew, I uh talked with Buck Paring, my sales manager, and I tried for you. I am on your side. He understands your situation, but he is tough. I can sell you this car for $40,500. That's a good price; these are great vehicles and they are just not staying around the floor very long before someone picks them up. That's a great offer from Buck, he's tough, but I think he really wants to see you drive out of here with that SUV. I don't think you are going to find this vehicle, with all these options for that price anywhere else. Can we earn your business? Need time to talk?"

That's Jerry. Most of the time he would come back with a frown and say that. Sometimes he puts a happy face on as if he has scored a big victory bickering for you with his own boss. So, let's break Jerry's words down. Is it important that he is on your side? Is it a relief to you that Buck has a soft spot for you? If you are Ted, you would be justified in feeling a little creepy right now. Is it a signal that these cars are not staying on the floor long; is this a signal that you should fish or cut bait right now? Are you happy Buck wants you to be happy? Again, watch it here Ted. Do you have confidence that this price is about the best anywhere for a comparable car?

Pop quiz over. The answer is almost always "NO" to all of these questions. There are exceptions to every rule – I am a lawyer after all and we thrive on exceptions – and sometimes some of these may be close to being true. But ordinarily, all of these things should not scare you or impress you. Jerry is not on your side. He is not working against you, really, he wants to sell you that car maybe as much or more than you want it. But Jerry has his own agenda, his own rules. He is trying to fit you into his rules. Dana is trying to do the same. Dana and Jerry are similar, but they are not on the same side. Do you really think Jerry is arguing with his boss on Dana's behalf? If Dana does, she should buy the car immediately. Ted should shake hands and get the heck out of there!

Actually, Ted likely has nothing to worry about. Buck does not have a soft spot for Dana, or Ted or anyone else he doesn't know except through Jerry. Buck does want you to be happy, so does Jerry, but on their terms; just like Dana wants them to be happy on her terms.

I have never had a salesman tell me or my wife or my dad that they just can't sell these cars and they are wasting away on their lot. Even when my wife and I bought a car that had been in the news because it was accelerating mysteriously at highway speeds, the salesman did not admit that they could not sell these cars because of the purported defect. We knew differently. I personally thought that a car that was so well engineered that it wanted to go even faster was not a bad thing at all. Sometimes cars do leave the dealer's lot very quickly. And there is the exception to the rule. But, whether the car you are buying is in demand or not, Jerry won't ever admit the latter. He will lower his price more ultimately, though.

Any salesman can tell you his dealership is the best. If he didn't think that way, he would not keep his job long. None of us would. If you really want to know whether Jerry's offer is the best out there, take out your cell phone and start calling. I doubt you will be able to dial seven numbers before Jerry tells you why that is a bad idea. Unless you actually do go to other dealers and talk about specific cars, neither you nor he will ever know if a competitor will beat Jerry's offer. You can certainly shop around after you get Jerry's (or Buck's) best offer. More on that later. So what did Jerry say that sent you any meaningful signal? What should you have heard from his pitch?

Maybe it was what Jerry did not say that was most important. Jerry said he would sell you that car for $40,500. He did not say that was his bottom line. He did not tell you to "go fish", or "take it or leave it." He essentially told you that $40,500 was simply his next offer.

When Jerry said that Buck "really wants you to drive out of here with that SUV" he was telling you that no matter what you think of the offer, don't walk away just yet. Jerry wants to keep talking if he has to. He is not done, and you don't have to be either. Lastly, he asked whether Dana and Ted needed time to talk. Why? Because he is implicitly inviting a counter offer. Take this offer, or talk it over and make a counter; Jerry can handle it.

One more thing. I am not impugning the integrity of Jerry or salesmen in general, but sometimes the "I talked to the boss" routine is just that; a ploy. Jerry may not have talked with Buck at all, at this stage. He may not talk to Buck until he has run out of his authority to decrease the price of the car. Yet, the car salesman's "need to talk further with his sales manager" before responding to your latest offer is very common with car dealerships. Inevitably, Jerry will likely see the need to talk with Buck, the man behind the curtain.

Maybe you just offered to buy the car for $37,000. So the salesman leaves you and takes his notebook of scribbles and numbers, and your most recent offer circled, ostensibly to go talk to the manager in the back of the office – the un-seen, all knowing and omnipotent, Wizard of Oz behind a curtain. A couple of things may be going on here. First, this is annoying, no other way to explain it. Maybe it is unique to car sales because it is so awkward that other businesses have not picked up on it. Unless the salesman is new and needs direction and counsel, the dealers really should be able to trust their salespersons to be able to negotiate a price with a customer. You should be able to trust the salesperson, and if they have to consult someone every time you make a new offer, your level of trust should go down dramatically. Why car dealers continue to use this sales manager ploy that really diminishes their salesperson's credibility is beyond this writer. But the truth is that this ploy is not new and it is not unusual and it is not reserved only for the newest salesperson.

I actually think that the sales manager is often used for two reasons. First, it gives the salesman an excuse to leave and strategize his next move in the negotiation. It gives him the chance to let you wait and wonder what his next move will be and to think about whether you want to increase your offer more, or maybe to wander around the showroom and fall more in love with the car. Use this time to talk with your spouse or whoever else may have an interest in buying the car. What will you do next, what is your strategy when he comes back and hopefully decreases his demand. Don't worry about whether the salesman is actually talking with a manager, it shouldn't affect your strategy. Sometimes the salesman may consult a manager, sometimes he may not, and sometimes I suspect that there is no manager even on duty. I have never seen a group of salesmen, notebooks in hand, lined up in front of an office waiting to see the Wizard.

The second reason that the salesperson uses this ploy is to get you ready for their last ditch pitch to sell you the car; the arrival of the sales manager to present you with their bottom line, hard sell price – take it or leave it from the Wizard, the all knowing salesman who has been promoted to sales manager because he can assert a more authoritative spell over you to convince you to buy that car at their final offer. Needless to say, I am not an advocate of this even more annoying approach, but more on this a little later.

As long as the salesman keeps coming back, alone, with a new offer, they are not done talking (see the Chapter "Never Say Never, Almost" later on). So keep talking. In fact, I do not recommend assuming that the sales manager will actually make an appearance. You may be able to negotiate your deal with the salesman without any hard sell. It may not be the dealer's policy to have a manager sweep in at the end. Despite the possibility that a manager might appear, negotiate with your salesman as if he has the authority to make the deal. But don't be surprised if the Wizard makes an appearance.

Maybe there are at least three reasons for the appearance of the Wizard. First, the salesman may not think that you are really serious about buying the car and he or she wants to bring in the manager to make one last, hard sell offer that they think you should take and if you don't, no more wasted time. The second reason is that they do this virtually every time, with every serious negotiation because they believe that this is the best way to send the signal that this is their bottom line, the best price that they can do and they are doing it because they like you and want to sell you that car. Lastly, they may bring in the manager on an ad hoc basis, only when it appears that they may not be able to make the sale unless they make a show of how great a deal this is and how they are bending over backwards to earn your business. In any event, the Wizard will not talk with you for a long time. This is their "final" offer and if you take it great, if you don't, oh well. That is the impression that the manager will want to leave with you.

As you might be able to tell, I am not a big fan of this approach. It denigrates the trust and credibility that your salesman has tried to establish with you. Why cut the legs out from under your sales staff? That's a rhetorical question, I don't know why this is a good strategy. But it exists, and you will have to respond to it. You could express your righteous indignation at being approached by such a heavy handed manager when you thought that you were going to be able to buy the Ford from your salesperson. Dana Meriweather could say "I have never been so insulted in my life", which if true means she has really lead a great life. Dana and Ted could then walk away in a huff. They do not make another offer and show the dealership, and that manager, that they are willing to walk away. That will make Dana feel good, no doubt, and she will be the hit of the showroom for the ten seconds it takes Ted and her to walk out. But they won't buy that car if they do. There are plenty of other cars out there and plenty of other dealers, too. Walking away is really one of the only true weapons that you have in the car buying negotiation and being willing to walk away is leverage. Walking away is also surrender. The biggest problem is that so many dealers use this manager ploy, you may run right into a different Wizard at the next dealer down the street. It's your choice, but being the hit of the showroom is not your goal, no matter how good it will feel.

You could walk out and then call your salesman in a day or two and make another offer to him – distancing yourself from the manager. This will make your salesman feel good, and give him the idea that he might end up with a sale after all. If you offer something close to the amount that the manager gave you, you might be successful. But remember that often the sales manager's job is to deliver their bottom line. So, the dealership has essentially backed themselves into a corner by telling you that the least they would sell you that car for was $X. If you ask them to take less, they would lose credibility if they accepted it. There is a chapter later on about Saving Face. But, if you don't accept the bottom line demand of the dealer at the time it is made, or after you have theatrically left the building and called back later, you may not be able to buy that car. Sometimes negotiations just don't work.

If the demand being made by the Wizard is within your comfort zone, is within the amount of money you are willing to pay for that car, don't diss the Wiz. Shake his hand and accept the offer, buy your car. Again, this is not an unusual strategy among car dealers and if the manager has emerged with his last great demand, this may mean that you wore them down as far as you could.

I recently negotiated to buy a car with my wife and I did not expect to see the manager. We were close numbers wise and I was confident we would be able to negotiate the sale with the salesperson alone. But there he was, the sales manager, with his last offer – their bottom line. I don't recall what that figure was, maybe $16,500 if I recall right. I had been offering $16,000. I shook his hand and said I was surprised to see him since I thought his salesman and my wife and I had been doing just fine without him. When he demanded $16,500, I indicated (grunted, probably) that that was more than I really wanted to spend, but if he could go to $16,250 we would take it. He did. Actually, $16,500 would have been fine, too, but I admit I was annoyed that they brought in the sales manager. I did not think that a counter offer would nix the deal. He could have said no and I would have then agreed to his $16,500 (lest I be shot on site by my wife).

The point is that you can take the righteous indignation approach to the appearance of the manager, but you don't have to. If their bottom line is within your acceptable range, suck it up and take it. You are the winner, remember; you bought the car for a price that you wanted. If you want, there is nothing wrong with making another counter offer one last time; even when the dealer says that is the last demand, that doesn't mean you can't try for a little better deal. While unique, these manager-type situations are not only found in car sales, though.

Often, negotiators do not have the final authority. A lawyer has his client, after all, and a salesman his boss or owner. Sometimes the negotiator will need to consult with their client or boss during the negotiations. Often, the salesperson or negotiator will have the authority to close a deal up to a certain point, but will need further approval for additional authority. If a negotiator continues to excuse himself or herself to "talk with" a higher up, it may be just a ploy or a bluff. Until a sales person or negotiator has exhausted his authority, there is no reason to have the boss or client approve every single move in the negotiation. So when the boss or the sales manager rushes onto the scene, the dealer is sending a signal that they are very near the end of their rope; or near the lowest that they are willing to sell you that car for at that moment. They may have one move left. But they are saying that they are either as low as they will go, or they are betting that they don't have to go any lower to sell YOU that car that day. It is a signal, a big one, and you need to recognize it.

The variations of signals that the other side in a negotiation sends you are impossible to list. What you need to know is that experienced negotiators mean what they say. Whether they are selling a new Ford or Cadillac or negotiating a construction contract, every word they say has meaning. They should not speak without the intent that what they say will have an impact on you or your next action. They don't say things that don't mean anything. If they say that they don't have much room left, they are telling you that they are not done negotiating and trying to signal that you need to get close to their number. If they were done, the salesman would tell you he did not have any rope left. If they mention a specific number, it is because they WILL accept it not because they can't. Words matter and listening to what your "opponent" is saying can be one of your greatest weapons. Be in a position to read the smoke signals that the other side is sending you.

You also have to be able to send some smoke signals of your own.

CHAPTER 10

RULE NUMBER VI, LEARN TO SEND YOUR OWN SMOKE SIGNALS

Your goal is to buy that car, sign that contract or settle that lawsuit for your price. You know where you want to be and are reasonably sure your price is fair, but you are still not there. In a world of perfect information you and your counterpart would not have to dance around the final price.

In a perfect world, that car salesman would honestly show you what that car cost them and all of the other variables that affect their bottom line: how the floor plan affects the precise car you are looking at; how long it has been on the lot; the cost to keep the car on the lot every day; their overhead costs; the incentives from the dealer for selling you that car. The salesman would let you know what they would expect in profit and let you know their absolute lowest price.

On the other hand, in this perfect world you would tell the salesman how much you could really afford. You would tell the salesman everything: the raises you expected in the future; your checking and savings account balances; the real reason you want to trade in your five year old car (leaky oil and a failing transmission); upcoming expenses that will affect your ability to pay more for a car at this point; the proceeds from your new book you are expecting, or the proceeds from the sale of an old family cabin that you are about to receive. You would honestly tell the salesman why you like the car, why you want to buy it, why you need to buy it and how much you are willing to pay; the most that you are willing to pay, regardless of what the dealer is willing to do.

If you are willing to pay more for the car than the dealer needs, that's ok! The dealer will get the extra money as profit. You have bought the car for what you were willing to pay, so you should be happy, shouldn't you? What if the dealer's bottom line is still higher than your top dollar? Well, you are out of luck, unless you want to pay more or the dealer feels sorry for you and will meet your price, at their loss, because of your honesty! If that were to happen, it means that they have made plenty of profit off of other people's honesty that week.

In real life, this simply does not happen. Maybe buying a car or a house, or negotiating that union contract, would be a whole lot easier if it did. So would life if we all just trusted one another and spilled whatever beans we had in a given situation. The result would be great in some cases, disastrous in others. Disastrous for those who were being honest but whose adversaries were not. They would be taken advantage of, often and horribly. So we allow people to negotiate better or worse deals. We let the market work out the kinks.

There is no question that some people simply pay more than others for the same car. There is no question that the same dealership will sell identical cars for less money to different people. This is a result of differences in power, imperfect market conditions and information, outside market factors and negotiating skill. We can help control the latter factor. Perfect honesty among negotiators is the exception and not the rule in life. It is also a utopia, a best case scenario that rarely happens. Yet, most economists will say that when left to an "arm's length" negotiation, the price for a given commodity will reflect all of these variables or factors. So, how do you get to be one of those folks who buys that Ford Edge in your price range; one of those folks who doesn't get taken to the cleaners so others can pay less? You do so by sending the right smoke signals at the right time.

First of all, you can't be wedded to reaching an agreement, buying that car no matter what. The Ted Meriweathers of the world need to listen to this. The first signal that you need to send in any negotiation is that you don't have to agree to anything. You are not desperate. You don't need this particular car, or house, or contract. In fact, if you make a deal just to avoid a conflict or to avoid walking away empty handed, it's not likely to be a good deal for you. You do not want to send the message that no matter what, you will buy that car, or make a deal. You cannot send the message that you really want that car and won't walk away without it.

If you send that signal, you will buy that car; it's an easy negotiation for you, an easy sale for the salesman. He will make sure that you buy that car, at a higher price than you could have paid for less of a car. The message that you need to send is that there are plenty of cars you can buy and if the salesman can't meet your price, you are more than willing to walk away. This puts pressure on the salesman to try and satisfy you now – so you don't walk away.

That car salesman is doing the same thing, of course. He reads books like this, attends sales seminars. He or she wants to send the message that he does not need to make this particular sale. He wants to send the signal that there are plenty of folks just like you who would love to buy this fine automobile. The fact is that neither one of you can afford to send a signal that no matter what, this car is going to be sold, or that this contract will be signed. In the context of buying a car, that means that you have to avoid letting your emotions run the show.

Now that the Meriwethers are sitting down in Jerry Wholesale's office or cubicle, what signals should they or can they send to Jerry? What should Dana do or say? Most of the discussion in any negotiation ultimately focuses on money. How often have we heard that a union is on strike and the main issue is health care or working conditions, only to find out later that the dispute was ended when the parties reached an agreement on wages? The answer is plenty; it's almost always about money.

Dana needs to be able to suggest to Jerry the price range that she and Ted will accept. She does that by sending signals to Jerry, without necessarily committing to any price too quickly. There are several ways to send these smoke signals.

Tell Jerry directly, don't beat around the bush; "I might be able to pay $38,000 or so, but I can't pay near what you are suggesting." Or, "We could see $37,000 or $38,000, but not what you're asking." But be careful. Dana doesn't want to signal the family's bottom line too soon (see Chapter 11 about splitting the difference). If Dana really wanted to buy the car for $38,000 and that is her bottom line, I would not suggest $38,000 as the first signal. Aim lower. Also, remember our previous rule; NEVER suggest a number that you cannot accept. If Dana gives a range of $37,000 to $38,000, she better be willing to buy that car for $38,000, no exceptions.

Always leave yourself some rope, especially early on in a negotiation. Suggesting a range – signaling an amount you could live with – is designed to get the salesman to do the same thing, signal where he or she wants to end up. If you can figure out what the other side's bottom line is, you can determine if you can buy the car and your strategy going forward becomes much easier. And remember, the salesperson should be doing the same thing, sending you a signal of where he wants to end up, but it shouldn't be his bottom number. He wants to leave himself some rope too. Having rope left is a good thing; that means neither one of you are done.

You don't have to be so direct, especially early on. We will get into this in the next chapter, but sometimes you can let the other side know that if you are going to buy that car, the price has to be closer to your number than the salesman's. That is particularly effective if your number is less than halfway between your current positions. Or express a number hypothetically; "If you could get to $37,000 I would not have to think about it, you've got a sale." If Dana says this, Ted may fall off his chair thinking "Honey, that's way too low. Jerry can't sell us that awesome car for $37,000." This is why we don't focus on Ted in this book.

Dana's statement puts pressure on Jerry, especially if that number is close to the dealer's bottom line. Jerry will say that is just not doable, not in the ballpark, "but if you want me to, I can take it to my manager and see what he says." Dana has provided a low number, but a number that tells Jerry she (and the by now un-conscience Ted) are willing to buy that car tonight. Dana does not really expect Jerry or the invisible Wizard to accept her offer, but it starts the negotiation and gives Jerry a number that he has to respond to. Jerry doesn't want to be too rude because he doesn't want Dana to walk out of the showroom. Jerry knows that if Dana walks out, the chances she will come back and buy a car go way down.

While most negotiations ultimately resolve based on money, there are other signals you need to be sending, too. You need to point out why your valuation of the car, or the house, or the contract, etc. is more accurate than the salesperson's. Point out why you don't think that car is worth what they are asking. Maybe it has higher miles, a dent here, a spot on the seat there, or maybe this new car is the last of the old style, shortly to be replaced by the new and improved version. Point out that the house you are trying to buy is not worth more than the house down the street that sold for $10,000 less. Let the plaintiff's lawyer know that his client's lawsuit is not likely to result in a big jury verdict, maybe it would result in nothing at all. Pointing out the merits of the subject of the negotiation sends the signal that you have done your homework and know what you will accept and why, you are not just shooting from the hip. It also gives you the chance to send additional hints about what you would accept, what you would pay,

Politicians sometimes use a trial balloon to test a particular policy. They float an idea in the public domain just to gauge the reaction to it. You can do the same in a negotiation. Suggest that you could see paying a premium for a similar Ford Edge if it had certain, additional options (bigger engine, towing package, sunroof, massive stereo system to rival any 17 year old's). Or suggest that you could see paying a little more if the dealer threw in some perks that you know the dealer has control over. Once again, the number you suggest has to be one you could live with and you need to leave yourself some rope.

The trial balloon can help reinforce your argument that your number is a more accurate reflection of the value of the car than the salesman's. It also lets the salesperson know that you are still willing to talk and that the number or numbers that you have been suggesting are still in play.

A word to the wise, however. The person on the other side of your negotiation may have read this book or may be very experienced in negotiating. They know the rule: Everything you say will prompt an equal and often opposite reaction from the other side. If Dana tells Jerry that she could buy that car for $10,000 less from another dealer, Jerry may just check it out. Bluffing is a very dangerous game, one that should not be played. If Dana really could buy that car for that much less, why isn't she talking to another dealer? People are not stupid, and they [should] listen to everything you say. After all, if you were Jerry and read the previous chapter, you would be listening to everything Dana is saying, right?

When you float any number, you are stuck with it. If Dana suggests she would buy that car for $38,000 and she later refuses to pay it when Jerry says he would sell at that price, her credibility is shot. Most good salesperson's who are not afraid of making their quota, would show Dana the door quickly and assume that she and Ted never were serious about buying a car. Then the salesman would see Ted weep and know he was mistaken.

Words mean something in negotiations, and every word or phrase that you use will evoke a reaction and can be relied upon. So if you talk about a fact, you need to make sure that you have it right. If you even float a price hypothetically, it needs to be acceptable. After all, your purpose in posing a hypothetical is to get the salesperson to respond to it favorably, isn't it? It doesn't make any sense to use a hypothetical that you wouldn't agree to, does it?

Let's talk about the options on a car again. We know that with new cars, there are hundreds of variations of bells and whistles that affect the price of a car. These variations are the "facts" of the new car sale. Whether a particular car you are talking with the salesman about has or doesn't have these options affects the desirability and the price of the car. The facts of a lawsuit are the proof that can be presented at trial; the product or service being offered are the facts of a contract negotiation. The more you know about what you are negotiating, the easier it will be to trade off one fact for another.

Compare the lack of a bell or whistle on the car you are negotiating about with the bell or whistle on a similar car. Point out sales advertisements of other dealers who are selling comparable cars for less than the salesperson is offering. Take the opportunity to suggest additional bells and whistles - like new, expensive floor mats or upgraded stereo installation - the salesperson could throw in to make a higher price acceptable.

Knowing that the dealership has a costly floor plan, high rent or that the dealership might receive a bonus as a result of selling you a car is great information to have. If you have it, let the salesperson know that you have this information. It can be used to help the salesperson "save face" if it appears that he or she is at the end of their rope and you need to give them a reason to go against their principles. More on this in a later chapter.

The salesperson- Jerry - is likely to give you several reasons why what you have pointed out are not really important. Jerry will deny that selling you this car will evoke a bonus, after all they can sell this car to someone else tomorrow for more money. Jerry will claim that his dealer needs a decent profit margin regardless of their floor plan or how long the car has been on the lot and, in fact, since this car is eating up interest, they have to get even more for it. Don't be intimidated. The dealer's defending against what you have pointed out is likely validation of your information.

As you talk and point out various aspects of the car or the dealership, you are sending the signal that you have done your homework. Even if Jerry has an answer for what Dana brings up (Jerry has heard it all before, most likely) he knows that she is serious and is not just throwing numbers around. Dana and Ted have done their homework and know what they will pay for their car and why. That is an important signal to send, and it increases Dana and Ted's credibility. The Danas and Teds of the world put themselves in a better position to be successful.

As Dana gets closer to her final number, there are additional signals that she can send. Assuming that Dana has saved some rope after she and Jerry have exchanged a couple of demands and counter offers but Dana has not offered all she has, she should let Jerry know that she can increase her offer but the final sale price has to be closer to her number than his. That tells Jerry that she will buy the car at a little below half of the difference between where they are presently. That is a perfectly good signal to send and stays clear of a specific number, IF TRUE. If Dana will buy that car for a little less than half way between her current offer and Jerry's last demand, she should say so. If not, she SHOULDN'T. Playing around with words or signals is not bargaining; it's lying.

Dana could tell Jerry that she will pay $38,000, and might be able to go a little higher if needed, but that's it. She is near the end of her rope. This lets Jerry know Dana is almost done, but leaves her room to increase her offer at least one more time.

What if Dana is just about out of money at $38,000 but Jerry has been slow to decrease his offer and is still above $40,000? Maybe Ted was right; this particular vehicle can't be bought for under $40,000. If Dana is not in a position to accept half of the difference between $38,000 and $40,500, she should not suggest it. You need to send realistic, truthful signals. If you are about at the end of your rope, the best thing for you to do is to admit it and let the salesperson know why. She should tell him that she and Ted can't see buying that car for any more than $38,000, maybe $39,000. She and Ted just don't have the budget for it and if Jerry can't let the car go for that price, they will just look elsewhere. Maybe Dana could let Jerry know they might be able to buy it for a little more, a couple hundred or so, but that is it. Or, if the dealer throws in a couple of sub-woofers and floor mats, maybe Dana and Ted could pay $39,500.

What if Jerry is telling Dana that he is at the end of his rope at $40,500? Dana and Ted do have a couple of options. Remember, unless and until Jerry says that is it, final offer, take it or leave it, Jerry and the so-far invisible Buck the manager have probably left a little rope in case they need it. But, Dana and Ted can always walk away. Send the message that they are not kidding; they are willing to walk away from that Ford Edge and look elsewhere. That may be the glue that keeps Jerry talking – his fear that Dana will walk out the door and statistics say Dana is not likely to come back. A good salesman will let you walk. Especially if he really was near the end of his rope. If Jerry was not at the end of his rope, he has made a mistake and will probably talk like hell to get Dana to sit back down. He probably won't have too tough of a time convincing Ted to sit down, if Ted even stood up.

Dana and Ted can always come back later. Rather than appear to be begging, Jerry can call Dana later and acquiesce. Neither is likely. There are other cars, and there will be other buyers, eventually.

Dana can suggest that the dealership throw in other options so she can increase her offer or pay their price. I mentioned this above. It works, but it is actually a "reverse saving face" maneuver that we will cover later. On the other hand, if you really want that car and the salesman is telling you "take it or leave it," you can always decide to take it. There is another aspect to the final price that is somewhat unique to the car buying process; the monthly payment.

Some buyers are more concerned with the monthly payment necessary to buy that new car than the bottom line price. Dana is not, but it is a concern for her and Ted. I think putting a lot of emphasis on the monthly payment as a buyer is a mistake that people make and one that the salespeople are all too eager to exploit. But if you are more concerned with the monthly payment, maybe you can have the life of the loan extended to lessen the monthly payments. The cost of this compromise is acceding in our scenario to Jerry's higher sales price and the higher interest fees. The dealership gets their money up front, with a discount for the present value of the income stream and a premium for the chance that you won't pay and the loan company takes the risk. You pay more for the car in the end, and that is really not the purpose of your negotiation or this book. But it is an option.

The same thing sometimes happens in a settlement of a lawsuit. If the plaintiff in a lawsuit agrees to accept a structured payout over a period of years, the person is likely settling for less cash up front. The present value of the income stream is less than the income stream; the present value is likely a compromise so that the total amount paid is satisfactory. Any negotiation takes into account the present value of the settlement.

In this chapter and in Chapter 9, we have talked about sending signals. Smoke signals. Smoke signals are what the American Indians were said to have used to communicate before the age of cell phones, text messages, or fax machines. The Indian Smoke Signals were non-verbal. There are non-verbal signals in negotiation that you need to listen to and learn to send, too. None of them involve fire.

When I am in trial, I always tell my client that he or she needs to maintain a poker face throughout the trial. As far as the jury was concerned, we expected every piece of evidence, good or bad, because we knew our case and were so confident of our position it didn't matter what anyone said on the witness stand. We were not surprised by anything. Most of my clients understood and complied.

Why poker faced at trial? Because I wanted to send a signal, a Smoke Signal to the jury that we were confident, competent and in control. Same thing in negotiations. How you react, what your body language says reveals a lot about what you are thinking. Sometimes you can send the wrong signal without saying a word. Sometimes you can send the right signal, subtly, with your reaction despite what you might be saying.

I love the TV car advertisement for Honda, I believe, where the buyer's alter ego literally sings the praises of the new Honda, finally exclaiming "we'll take it!" No negotiation necessary there, the price was apparently right. Only on TV. The buyer could have told the salesman in the ad that the price was just too high for his budget. But that little man on his shoulder clearly expressed the buyer's true feelings.

That little man on your shoulder is your smile, the shrug of a shoulder, the obvious exhale of stress in reaction to a counter offer. It is the disappointing shake of you head, the raising of your hands in surrender or the not so subtle rolling of your eyes. The way you react, physically, to the car salesman's comments to you send very important signals to him or her about what you are really thinking. Should you let the person on the other side of the negotiations know how you truly feel – or should you hide your true feelings?

Neither, necessarily. The fact is sometimes you want or need to convey your true feelings, other times you don't. Sometimes you want to reject the offer, but send a signal that you are close to being ready to pull the trigger. Sometimes you want to send the opposite signal; you want to indicate that you appreciate the fact that the salesman reduced his price, but deep down you aren't thrilled. The trick is simply to make sure that your body language is sending the Smoke Signal that you want to send – regardless of how you really feel.

So Dana has a lot on her plate with non-verbal smoke signals. First, she has to be sure that she is reacting the way she wants to react; not necessarily her true feelings of course, but how she wants Jerry to perceive her mood. Does she want to come off as frustrated at his most recent demand (hands on hips, the shake of the head, a soft sigh)? Does she want to convey that Jerry is close to a deal by emulating a silent "oooh", or a tilt of the head and nearly a smile? Does she want to point, as if the next thing she says should seal the deal.

Jerry is doing the same thing. He may be thinking that Dana's offer is not bad, very close to what his bottom line is. He may come back and shake his head, or put up his hands to send the solid signal that Dana is not on the right track. He might, though, encourage Dana by relaxing or nodding almost in agreement. Both Dana and Jerry have an agenda, a hidden one that they need to convey verbally and non-verbally.

Dana has another problem. It is almost that little man on her shoulder in the Honda commercial. It's Ted. Like a lawyer with a client, Dana does not want Ted to send a different signal than what she is trying to send. Ted could be obvious. He could verbally contradict her by telling Jerry that his price is good, his wife is just playing around needlessly. Not bright, but it could happen. He could insult Jerry, intentionally or unintentionally – like unknowingly berating his alma mater. Or, he could send an opposing non-verbal signal. He could zig when Dana is zagging. If Dana is trying to convince Jerry that he needs to come down closer to her number than his, or trying to finagle some new floor mats and undercoating, Ted could be silently applauding, or shaking his head as if to signal that Dana really doesn't mean what she is saying, they are ready to close the deal.

These sound like trivial matters, almost comical. But very often in a negotiation two is a crowd. When I tell my clients to maintain a poker face it isn't really because I don't expect to be surprised – I am often surprised. It is because I don't want my client to interfere with how the jury perceives us or our position in the case. If I thought that my clients could read my mind and mimic my thoughts with their reactions, there would be no reason for a poker face. If Dana could control Ted and be assured that he would not contradict her, she would not have anything to worry about. Most people can't control Ted, or husbands like him. Men don't understand women, so husbands can't control their wives either. If you are negotiating with someone else by your side, you need to make sure that you all know what the plan is. As we talked about in our previous chapter, have a plan, share it, and read from the same page of the plan. Jerry will not only be looking at Dana while they try and make a deal, he will be looking at Ted, too. If Ted is sending the wrong signal, Jerry will not overlook it. He will use it against Dana and Ted.

Thus, whether you are sending Smoke Signals verbally or non-verbally, you need to very carefully choose your words or act in a way that sends the message or the signal to your opponent that you intend. And there is nothing wrong with changing your strategy or signals as you get into the negotiations. If you can put yourself in a position to suggest that you and your salesman split the difference, you are well on your way to having your smoke signals returned favorably.

CHAPTER 11

RULE NUMBER VII, THE RULE OF 1/2 – SPLIT THE DIFFERENCE

I have been involved in negotiating settlements where the opening demand from an opponent exceeded $1 million. Eventually, these cases settled for much less. On the other hand, I have settled cases where the initial demand was $20,000 and the final settlement was as much as $15,000. Some negotiations are easier than others. But there is one rule that seems to work for both parties: The rule of ½.

Sometimes there is not a big difference between the original offer and the final number. Construction contracts in markets with standard wage rates and profit margins may not leave a lot of bargaining room. On the other hand, where the value of the commodity at issue is vague and fungible, the initial positions of the buyer and seller may not come close to resembling the final number. The parties will start very far apart, staking out their positions, slowly inching toward a final resolution.

Either way, the rule of ½ is a strategy more than a rule. The strategy is to put yourself in a position to tell the other side that you will split the difference between their present price and the price you are willing to pay. What can be more reasonable than telling them that you will meet them half-way? That is a signal that should be one big green light, shouldn't it? It is difficult for your opponent, your salesperson, to argue that inflicting pain on each other equally is outrageous, unconscionable or ridiculous – it's none of those things, is it? It's compelling, it's fair and reasonable all at the same time WHEN THE TIME IS RIGHT.

As negotiations progress, one side offers and the other counters. If you are buying a car, you may not be that far apart at the beginning. If you are negotiating a multi-million dollar contract, you could be hundreds of thousands of dollars apart for quite some time. You have a magic number, or at least a range of where you want to end up. In my experience, however, it is difficult to keep your number or range halfway between your and your opponent's offers all of the time. If both parties have evaluated the object of their desire the same, and have decided to negotiate in a similar manner, the negotiations will likely proceed quickly to that same number. Most of the time that doesn't happen.

Most of the time, the parties will trudge along without targeting your number right in between. As you negotiate, pay attention to how much your opponent is moving in relation to his previous demand. If the salesman comes back from his office and takes an additional $500 off of the price of the Ford Edge, you should him and haw, and offer $500 more, if that much. If the salesman is decreasing his demand at a slower rate than you are increasing yours, you may want to adjust your strategy.

That is because eventually, you want to put yourself in a position to tell your salesman that you are willing to split the difference – be fair and reasonable. More on that in a moment. Let's look at our hypothetical car sale with Dana, Ted and Jerry.

Let's assume that the sticker price of the Ford Edge that Dana and Ted have set their sights on is $45,000. Jerry tells Dana that he can let it go for $44,000. However, Dana would like to pay $41,000 (Ted is happy at $45,000, but does not voice his opinion). So Dana starts off with an offer of $35,000. That is likely very low, and Dana has no realistic chance at buying the car for that. She knows this (Ted is bewildered) but wants to bring Jerry down closer to earth sooner rather than later. Jerry visits the back room, after he has Dana sign beside the $35,000 figure to signify that she and Ted would buy the car at that price. It looks so official, but the exercise is meaningless. Jerry walks back to the proverbial sales office, not optimistic, but deliberately. Jerry then comes back after talking with his mythical manager ("Norm", who hangs out at Cheers) shaking his head certain that you have dissed a beautiful machine on wheels. He comes down to $43,500. What can Dana do?

Dana could offer a whopping $35,500, but at that rate she and Ted would not buy the car until the next model year. However, the midpoint between her offer and Jerry's new price is now $39,250 ($43,500 plus $35,000 divided by 2). That is lower than Dana's magic number of $41,000. If Dana continues to nickel and dime Jerry, he may just cut off negotiations and refuse to drop any lower – he may think Dana and Ted are not serious about buying a car but just like to talk about it.

Why not let the dealer know that after talking it over with Ted, Dana will offer $36,000, but if the salesman would split the difference at $39,000, they would buy it on the spot.

This puts the ball in Jerry's court to come up with a reason not to be reasonable and meet them half way. If Jerry comes back with a demand of $43,000, which would be logical, Dana is still at a position to split the difference between $43,000 and $39,000 at $41,000. Remember, when Dana said she and Ted would split the difference at $39,000, she essentially offered $39,000 – that's why you shouldn't jump to suggest $41,000 too soon. The truth is, if Dana low balled Jerry at $35,000, splitting the difference at $39,000 probably would not happen. Dana should wait another round before offering to split the difference. She could play around some more, discussing options and comparisons with other cars or other dealers to attempt to convince Jerry that the value of the car is closer to her number than his. Eventually though, Dana will want to be in a position to be willing to split the difference at her number, $41,000.

Does this mean that Jerry will actually agree to meet her in the middle? No, Jerry may not agree to that, ever. But, the goal for Dana is to give herself and Ted the best chance to end the negotiation at their number. That is always the goal with any game plan.

What if Dana's mid-point started above her $41,000 figure? What if Dana offered $39,000 initially, instead of $35,000 and Jerry said he would sell her the car for $44,500? Maybe Dana offered too much to begin with; maybe Jerry is playing it close to the vest. What does Dana do now?

The answer is that Dana simply needs to increase her subsequent offers at smaller increments than Jerry is decreasing his, explaining that her initial offer was quite generous and legitimate. The game is to get the negotiations moving in tandem with her number becoming squarely in the middle. Dana wants to be able to split the difference at $41,000, just as above.

Why does this rule of ½ work? It works because generally, people gravitate toward symmetry, whether in math, interior design, art or disputes. We are, perhaps sadly, most comfortable with moderation. Most people avoid conflict. Liberal politicians move to the center during the general election, conservatives move to the moderate side. Both want to be seen as moderate or reasonable, forget right or wrong.

So, too, it is with negotiations. Eventually, the potential resolution of the negotiation lies near the midpoint of the offers. Most people will attempt to guide the discussions to a "reasonable" conclusion, reasonable meaning a middle ground. No matter what side you are on, you should be working to put your number in the crosshairs of your negotiating positions.

It is a good feeling to be able to say that you are willing to meet your salesperson half way. You will be the reasonable one, the fair minded person and meet them in the middle. This puts you in a good negotiating position – it is logical and fair, if one looks at the raw numbers. It puts the salesperson on the defensive to explain why meeting in the middle is not fair. That is tough to do and gives you a good chance that you will be able to buy that car at your price. The only caveat is that while you should try to steer the negotiations toward that target in the middle, you do not want to offer to split the difference too soon. Once you do offer to split the difference, you have offered to buy the car for that amount and any offer for a lesser amount is not credible. When you do start to employ the rule of ½, always try to leave yourself at least a little rope. Think about making that number below your true bottom line to leave yourself with extra room to maneuver.

CHAPTER 12

RULE NUMBER VIII, BE WILLING TO WALK AWAY

Power often dictates what party will do better in a negotiation. How often have you ever negotiated over the terms or price of an insurance contract? Unless you are in a large corporation whose business is sought after by many insurers, the answer is never. The price and content of the policy is generally not negotiable. The losses that the company will insure for their price are the only variables that are discussed. You have no power in this situation, there is no negotiation. This book will not help you buy insurance. Your only option is to find another company who has a lower price for a comparable product. Your only option is to essentially walk away.

Where there is some give and take, it is important to determine what power you do have. If you own a business negotiating to build a new facility that will award a large construction contract occurring over a period of years, you have a lot of power. Construction companies will want to accede to your company's requirements to win the contract.

I don't often refer to civil lawsuits, because that's what I do. I don't want to give away any secrets and I can't breach any confidences. But in a civil lawsuit, a car accident say, the balance of power often rests with the underlying facts. A very sympathetically injured, innocent victim looks pretty good when compared with a corporate defendant whose driver was rushing back to work after lunch when the accident occurred. On the other hand, if the corporate defendant has a defense that has a good chance of winning and defeating the plaintiff's claim entirely, that party is in the driver's seat in a negotiation. No matter how deep the pocket, there is still the concept of responsibility.

In negotiation, parties use their power to fashion a deal in their favor. The result of negotiation is, by design, a compromise of what the parties each desire. It resembles and takes into account the relative merits of each side. It also has to reflect the power of each side's argument or position. The parties have to calculate their risk of loss and chance of success into their bottom line number or range of acceptable outcomes. So what?

In order for this power to be credible, the other side has to believe that you are prepared to allow the negotiations to fail if you don't get your way. Walking away and not agreeing at all may be your only leverage, or it may be just one of several options that you discuss. Nevertheless, you have to keep it in plain view of your opponent.

Perhaps the WORST signal you can send is that you will make a deal no matter what. That sounds odd. Who would do that? Plenty of people send that message, whether they know it or not. If you keep rambling on about how great that car is and how much you really want to buy it, you are telling your salesman that you will do what you have to in order to buy it. That is the wrong smoke signal.

The smoke signal you should be sending is that you are willing to walk away from the discussions; your principles are more important than agreeing just to agree. If you cannot buy that SUV for what you can afford, you SHOULD walk away. Despite any emotional attachment you have developed with the car, no matter how much you love it, be willing to walk out the door without it. The fact is that there are other dealers and cars are plentiful. Walking away from a new car salesman is a credible threat to the salesperson in front of you. The last thing Jerry wants is for Dana and Ted to walk away, because that dramatically decreases his chances of ever selling them a car. Yet, there are other buyers for that Ford Edge. Both sides to a negotiation have to send the same signal; sometimes a deal can't be made.

You need to show that salesperson that you will leave if you don't get what you want. That may make the salesperson work harder. My dad was an expert at buying cars. He was tough. I have seen him throw his hand up, declare that he can't do business, cordially shake the salesman's hand and walk away.

I used to wonder why he did that, really wanting him to buy that car. As children, we all resemble Ted don't we? I later realized that sometimes he did it to prove to the dealer that he could. He might call the salesman later to see if sentiments had changed, or the salesman might call him back. If he did not buy that car, he always found another. But I never saw him buy a car outside of his price range. He was good at evaluating cars and he was good at executing a negotiation strategy even if the negotiation did not succeed.

If you send the signal that you will buy that car, that house, settle that lawsuit or accept that contract no matter what, you can count on being taken advantage of. My dad never was taken advantage of when he bought a car. You don't have to be either.

I once represented a large, municipal corporation that will remain nameless in the purchase of a piece of property that cost nearly eight hundred thousand dollars or so, as I recall. The Secretary of the municipal corporation and I arrived at the title company late one afternoon to sign the paperwork. Lo and behold, the title fees were about ten thousand dollars more than what the sales documents had represented.

The Secretary objected and put on his coat; that was not the deal and he would not follow through with the sale. Over ten thousand dollars, a little over one percent, he was quite willing to risk vacating the sale altogether. He not only sent the signal that he would walk away, but he was on his way out the door. It was no bluff, but the real estate agents involved decided to eat the additional fees to save the deal.

Things don't always work out that way, of course. But negotiations don't have to result in an agreement; a compromise. You have to show the other side that you know this. **The best way to succeed in any negotiation is to be willing to**

fail, and make sure you let the other side know it. In the context of buying a car, this means being prepared to walk away. In terms of a union wage negotiation, it means being willing to strike, or willing to let the worker's strike or shut down the plant. There are other houses to buy. In litigation, it means being ready to try the case – let a jury decide the value of the claim or decide that it has no value. **Again, the best way to succeed in any negotiation is to be ready, willing and able to fail and to make sure the other side knows it.**

CHAPTER 13

RULE NUMBER IX, DON'T BE PENNY WISE AND POUND FOOLISH

Now that you are all excited, ready to go to battle and walk away in disgust if you don't get your way, let's take a deep breath. Rule Number VIII still applies, always. You have to be willing to not come to an agreement, to not buy that particular car. But you don't have to be too eager to walk away, either.

CAUTION: Don't use every one of these rules in every situation. Sometimes these rules are not compatible with each other. While you have to be willing to walk away, you also have to continually weigh the consequence of walking away.

In every negotiation, both sides are weighing compromise results. There are risks to each side in every negotiation. If you walk away from that dealership because you think the dealer should have met your price, there is no guarantee that you will be able to buy that car later. In fact, most of the time, the dealer will never call you back about that car. I called a dealer back once after walking away from our negotiations. I tried to offer a little more to buy the car, but he would not budge at all. In a home sale, the risk is that you will lose the sale if things break down. In a union contract negotiation, there is a risk of a strike if the talks are unsuccessful; the workers would be out of work, the business interrupted. In lawsuits, if negotiations fail a trial may result and each side risks losing. Let's look at another hypothetical – the case of the runaway boat.

Let's assume that a plaintiff sues a large corporation that makes an outboard boat motor because the plaintiff was injured when the ski-boat he was operating in neutral suddenly kicked into gear, knocking him out of the boat and into the water. His boat then ran over him causing severe injury. Plaintiff sued because he claims that the motor had a mechanical defect that caused the motor to spring into gear.

The outboard motor manufacturer, on the other hand, claims that a recent repair was the cause of the accident and that the anomaly was not found to be present in any of their other motors. Additionally, the corporation claims that the boat owner should have had the "kill switch" engaged at the time of the accident. A kill switch is a small rope that is worn on a boat operator's wrist or clothing and if the rope is stretched, it will shut off the motor. The plaintiff in our hypothetical did not wear it because it restricted his mobility.

In this case, both sides have plenty to argue about. The plaintiff was minding his own business on a warm summer day when the motor he spent so much money to buy, suddenly kicked into gear. He did not do anything to cause the accident, yet he is horribly injured and will need future surgery to keep him alive and he will need continued therapy. He can no longer work and his relationship with his wife is affected.

On the other hand, the boat motor company will have its experts testify that there was no defect in the motor when it left their assembly line. Their motors have never done this before. The motor company will be able to point to a repair that was made that they will say caused the motor to spring to life. Besides, had the plaintiff been wearing the kill switch on his boat, none of this would have happened.

These facts will be argued and factored into the parties' negotiations. But the reason why both sides would want to negotiate a settlement is that each side has a risk. We generally negotiate uncertainties, not known outcomes.

The plaintiff in this situation risks losing his case to a jury. The jury could agree that the accident was not the company's fault and award nothing. Or, they could award an amount less than his medical bills and or less than the amount of the corporations' best offer to settle, which would be a loss too. In either event, the plaintiff risks not being fully compensated for his injury. Wouldn't this encourage the defendant to take the case to the jury in the hopes that the jury will find it not liable?

Not necessarily. Because the jury might believe that the plaintiff simply did not deserve to be run over by his own boat. The jury could believe that the company should have manufactured a boat motor that did not change gears at will. The jury could award the plaintiff millions of dollars, if not tens of millions of dollars against the motor maker.

Thus, both sides face big, multi-million dollar risks. In other situations, the risks may not run into the millions of dollars, but risk nonetheless fuels each side's interest in coming to an agreement that takes into account these risks and eliminates them. That's why most cases settle before verdict. It is why car makers sell their cars for less (sometimes a lot less) than the sticker price; if they didn't, they may not sell enough and they don't want to lose a sale to a competitor.

So what happens when the plaintiff in our boating example evaluates his case as having a settlement value of between $900,000 and $1.1 million and demands $930,000 from the boat manufacturer? Plaintiff tells the manufacturer/defendant that he will not take anything less to settle the case. Meanwhile, the defendant boat motor company has come to the conclusion that the case is worth between $800,000 and $870,000, and have offered $850,000.

In theory, this runaway boat case should not settle. Both sides have presumably done their homework and evaluated how much they are willing to accept to resolve the case. Plaintiff's bottom line is $900,000, defendant's bottom line is $870,000. They should end up $30,000 apart, no deal, shouldn't they?

That is a lot of money to most of us, isn't it? That would just about buy our Ford Edge. It's enough money to stand firm on, in most cases. But in the scheme of things, in the context of our contrived example, it is only a difference of three percent. For the sum of $30,000 out of $900,000, the plaintiff is going to risk losing everything? For the sum of $30,000 out of a potential verdict in the millions, a defendant is going to roll the dice? Not many players on a TV game show would take those risks. Dana might, if she and Ted could afford the mother of all motor homes.

The risk of loss to each side is simply too great for either to throw down the gauntlet and try the case, unless there are egos involved, of course, which is appropriate for another book, not this one. There are costs associated with a trial to consider too. Those costs could equal or exceed $30,000 for each side. Logically, then, the three percent difference fades when compared with the risk and considering the cost of not resolving the case in negotiation.

But logic does not always accompany a negotiation. That's why we need this rule. **There is no virtue in absolute stubbornness**. Zero tolerance is a policy adopted by many school districts nowadays to address problems. It has led to disciplining girls for taking a Mydol and boys for drawing a picture of a stick man with a gun. Zero tolerance draws a line, no matter how illogical or divorced from an individual case that line may be. It is zero intelligence, really, because it says that teachers and administrators are not bright enough to make a decision as to what should be and what should not be a punishable offense.

Zero tolerance has no place in negotiations either. While you work toward realizing your goal, you have to reserve the flexibility to not draw a line just to draw a line. In our example, if the plaintiff rejects the settlement out of hand, he could go to trial and be awarded nothing. That is a huge risk. So is going to trial as a defendant who could have settled for around $900,000, but instead ended up with a verdict for the plaintiff of $5 million. Both would be doing so over a three percent variance from what they wanted, which was, after all, just an educated analysis of the discounted value of the risks involved. Each side would be penny wise and pound foolish to walk away from the bargaining table over three percent in this situation.

In our car buying example, the risk of a verdict is not present. Yet, there may be a point at which only a small difference separates Dana and Ted's goal from the dealer's bottom line; or separating a profit margin from another sale. The risk to Dana and Ted is that they have inaccurately estimated the value of the car and will never be able to buy a similar car at that price. Conversely, Jerry risks not being able to sell that car until another willing buyer comes along. The longer that takes, the more it costs his boss.

The point is that there is a point at which you are justified in compromising your goals and completing the sale, or settling the lawsuit, or executing the contract. That point will differ depending on the situation, but it will be the point at which it is silly to insist on your idea of reasonable. If the car dealers of the world did not understand this, they would go broke. If we car buyers didn't understand this, we'd be riding bikes.

CHAPTER 14

RULE NUMBER X,
NEVER SAY NEVER – ALMOST

This rule is not really related to not being penny wise and pound foolish. But too often we draw that final line in the sand, only to draw another one after it is crossed. Like the United Nations passing 50 or 60 resolutions, daring Saddam Hussein (remember him?) not to violate them or else. Or else what, he probably asked humorously. Or else the United Nations will pass another resolution that he better not violate. And they did so, time and time again. What did the resolutions mean after they were violated and not enforced? Nothing. It was clear to Iraq at the time that the UN really didn't mean it when they said "this is the last time."

How often have you said to your spouse or your children, "this is my final offer," only to offer something more? If you did, you have violated this rule of negotiation. Don't, I repeat don't say that you are done negotiating, this is your bottom line, this is your final offer UNLESS YOU REALLY, REALLY, REALLY MEAN IT.

I think there are some people who operate under the opposite rule. Make every offer, from your first to your last, the final offer, the line in the sand. That works the first time the other person hears it. The person on the receiving end of the first final offer believes, for a fleeting moment, that you really might have offered the farm from the get-go and there isn't any more corn in the silo. So they counter offer anyway, reluctantly.

And . . . you draw another line. "Ok, you got me. My real final offer is X." After a couple more rounds of negotiating like this, the cat is out of the bag. You really don't mean it. When you say "this is my final offer" that really means "I'm not done yet." That's not a good strategy.

Rules Number V and VI encourage sending signals to the other side. The only way you can effectively send a credible signal is to be true to your word. That's how signals work. In fact, if there is one characteristic that all negotiators need to have it is credibility. Credibility is why you never mention a figure or a position that you would not be willing to accept.

The best approach regarding your final offer is to not say that you have offered your top dollar until and unless you have done so. You should only make one final offer. You can certainly push for your position or a particular price vigorously at any time, but there is really only one final offer. Once you say that you are done, you will lose credibility if you continually go back on your word. Once you say that you are done, you have backed yourself into a corner.

If you only negotiate with a person on one occasion, for that new Ford Edge for instance, you will probably get away with drawing more than one line in the sand. Dana could make a "final offer", telling Jerry Wholesale that "$40,000 is as much as Ted and I can pay. That's my final offer." If she does so, she will have to tell Ted and the kids not to shake their heads in disgust, but what if Jerry comes back and says his invisible sales manager will go $40,250? Dana could wait for this invisible soul to make an appearance and try again at $40,000, or ask for another split of the difference. Or, she could tell Jerry she and Ted will take it if they throw in the premium floor mats, or throw in the front seat headrests with the rear facing T.V. screens. Dana will likely not see Jerry again, so if he is upset or perplexed by her strategy he will get over it. But if Dana faces the prospect of buying another car from him, she will fare much better if she follows this rule. Dana should be very careful before laying down the gauntlet.

In fact, following this rule will help you reach your goal, to buy that Ford in your price range. If you have the deserved reputation of being a straight up, credible negotiator, your counter-part will believe you when you tell them this is your final offer. So often we are trying to buy that car, or that motorcycle at the lowest price we can. How often after we have bought our car have we wondered whether the salesman would have actually sold it to us for less? If Dana is like most of us, she will be listening to her friends' car buying stories and looking at the newspaper ads for some time trying to see if she got the best deal she could have. Ted won't be, and Ted is the smart one after the deal is done.

Could we have bought that house for $300,000 instead of $305,000? Could we have convinced the customer to pay another $500 or so for that new back deck, or kitchen remodel if only we would have held out for more? If we believe that we didn't sell our car for the highest price, we are depressed. If we think that we could have bought that car for less, we feel cheated! Of course, if you bought that house or car within your well-reasoned range of acceptability, you shouldn't look back. You succeeded. If you sold your house or car for the amount you needed, you won.

So, when you tell the Ford dealer that this is all you have to offer, this is your last offer take it or leave it, you are essentially telling him or her that you are at the end of your range, he has sold you that car for the highest amount that you will accept. That tells the salesperson that it is ok for him or her to take the deal, he has worked you down to your bitter end; he has done the best he could have done. In our scenario, when Dana says that is it, Jerry has a decision to make; should he accept that he has gotten Dana and Ted to accept the most that they were willing to pay (a win for him), or is their offer really a little too short for his dealer to make the sale. That's Jerry's decision; the ball is in his court. Yet, Jerry is more likely to accept Dana's final offer when she has credibility when she says it.

The opposite is true, of course. The salesperson who credibly tells the customer "this is the absolute best we can do for you, we can't sell this car to you for any less" has the best chance of closing the sale. When and if Jerry says this to Dana, he is telling her that she has won, she has negotiated the lowest price for that Ford Edge that she could have negotiated. The ball is in her court. Can she accept this victory, or is the demand still above the price range she and Ted had settled upon?

Is all of this to say that negotiating is really a race to be the first to say "take it or leave it?" Not necessarily, but as the negotiations wind down, over the course of an hour or a little more in the car dealership, or over days or weeks or more in union negotiations, someone will say it and someone will be on the other end of it. The trick is to be careful when you are the one laying down the gauntlet. The only way you can gain trust and credibility when negotiating with strangers (which is who most of us negotiate with 99% of the time) is to be truthful in your dealings with them. That is true throughout the negotiations, right up to your final offer.

A good negotiator will simply mean it when they say that they have made their final offer. Jerry may not ever say it to Dana, he might bring out his sales manager to do so. Dana may never get to that point because Jerry and company may not ever offer an amount that they are willing to accept. But either way, if Dana or Jerry or the manager says this is it, they better mean it. Car dealers know this, most of them do anyway.

So what do you do when the dealer tells you this is it, this is all that we can do, the lowest we can sell you that car for? If you are Ted, maybe you say "Jeez, we are so close! Honey why don't we just give in and buy the car from this nice man." If so, you are done, read no further. And Ted, no need to stay at home tonight, I doubt Dana will mind if you stay at the Comfort Inn for a day or two, or maybe longer. But if you are not Ted, read on.

You are perfectly justified in testing Jerry's statement by suggesting other solutions or continuing to make counter offers. Dana can ask to split the difference, again. She could ask for additional options that the dealer could add to sweeten the deal. But if Jerry is truly at his last offer, what does she do?

Dana could and should accept the offer if it is within her and Ted's price range. If not, she can begin to alter other parts of the object of the negotiation that may not be part of his "final offer." Dana could let him know that is more than she and Ted ever wanted to pay, but they will buy it at that price if the dealer adds floor mats, or an undercoat, or some other option that is important to Dana and Ted, but not essential to the dealer. Maybe the dealer will provide free gas or change the payment terms, lower the down payment required. In any event, if Dana can cause the conversation to focus on her acceptance of Jerry's price, she may be able to change other aspects of the purchase to make it more acceptable to her and Ted – but leave the dealer with his final offer intact. Leave Jerry feeling that he has won. Remember that.

So what is Rule Number X? Only make one final offer. Sounds simple, but it really isn't in practice. If it appears that you or your counter-part have made your final offer, what in the world can you do to make violating it acceptable? You can employ Rule number XI.

CHAPTER 15

RULE NUMBER XI, SAVING FACE

Pride and dignity. These are grand emotions that have caused great care to be used when arranging chairs and providing food in some negotiations. Especially in international matters. No need to offend one party and distract the business at hand. Vanity also plays a role. The truth is that no one wants to be shown up. You want to not only resolve your issue, or buy that house or car, but you want to walk away believing that you came out ahead. The dirty little secret is that you want to feel like you won the negotiation. Everyone does. You want to believe that you were able to buy that Ford SUV for less money than your neighbor would have. Don't worry, your salesman wants to believe that he sold you that car for more than you would have paid at a competitor's dealership. It is human nature. We want to win!

So paradoxically, you want your counterpart to believe that he or she has won the day! This is not a novel concept. Dana and Ted can worry so much about winning themselves that they forget that Jerry is in a race to win too. If Jerry does not feel like he has won, Dana and Ted may drive home in their old car. Dana should want Jerry to believe that he has sold her that car at a higher price than she or Ted wanted to pay – regardless of what she and Ted were thinking when they walked in the door. And Jerry will be congratulating Dana on her negotiation skills if he sells her the car because he wants her to feel that she got a good deal. It may seem a little childish and archaic given our information society in which secrets are vanishing on the internet, but it is reality. We want to win but in order to do so, we have to make sure that the other side believes they won too.

So resist the temptation to regale your salesman or your friends with how you really bought that car cheap. No victory dances, no excessive celebrations in the dealer's parking lot. Your salesman should not genuflect either. You can both be satisfied with the outcome, and both be winners. After all, if you want your car salesman to accept your offer, you need to convince him that your price is a good deal for him, not that it is a good deal for you.

So what if Dana and Ted are back in Jerry's office and he comes back with his last, best offer of $40,250. Take it or leave it. Besides calling his bluff and going to another dealer, is there anything else Dana might be able to do to bring his number down that $250 or so that they need to fit within their range? We talked about adding some items to the deal in the last chapter. If Jerry knows that he and Dana are only $250 apart, he may be willing to throw in some additional items to make her feel as if she succeeded in buying the car for her price.

There is another way to look at the situation. Once Jerry has said that $40,250 is the dealer's last offer, he has backed himself into a corner. He will look bad (lose credibility) if he then lowers his offer. Nobody wants to look bad.

How many of us recall telling a boyfriend or girlfriend that we want to break up, it's over, only to regret it the next day? How do you go back to him or her and say you've changed your mind, you want them back? The answer is, in most cases, you either don't ever go back because you would look really, really bad, or you do a mea culpa; "I was just kidding" and they ask you "why?" What has happened since yesterday that causes you to want to get back together now?

Great question. Not a lot of good answers most of the time and it explains why it is so hard for both sides to go back to the way things were after one has drawn the line. It is the same in negotiations. It is difficult to continue negotiating when one side has drawn a line in the sand. The solution to the dilemma is found in the seemingly rhetorical boyfriend/

girlfriend question. Relax Ted, I am not saying that Jerry and Dana have become an item.

But if Jerry has drawn a line in the sand, Dana needs to provide him with a new reason to justify his lowering his offer one more time. She needs to let him take something new into consideration that justifies his violating his final offer without losing credibility. Dana needs to let Jerry save face.

Dana can point out an aspect of the sale or a characteristic of the car that she and Jerry may not have discussed previously. She can point out that a competitor priced a similar car in a newspaper ad at or below Jerry's price. Or maybe the car being considered has a smaller motor than comparable vehicles, or the interest rates just went up increasing her cost and decreasing the cars value in the future. Maybe there is a blemish on the interior of the car (a stain, or bad stitching) that she can bring up as a reason that Jerry should decrease his offer. Maybe Dana could increase the down payment she and Ted were offering, if that would help.

The concept of saving face is not something discussed overtly. No one tells his negotiating partner, "I am telling you this so you can save face and not look foolish." If you do that, I would predict an abrupt (albeit cynically comical) end to the negotiations. Yet, this notion of saving face exists on both sides.

Broadly speaking, you cannot let your counterpart believe that he or she has been beaten down in the process. You need to provide your opponent with a new reason to accommodate you and remain successful in the process. You have to remember that both you and your counterpart eschew looking bad. That is one of the unspoken rules of the game.

CHAPTER 16

THE THRILL OF VICTORY AND THE AGONY OF DEFEAT

These rules work. You don't have to use every one of them every time. No one uses all of the keys of a piano to play every song. You use the keys that fit and finish the song, that's all. Sometimes you hit a wrong key, too. Sometimes you aren't able to buy that car, despite following the rules. These are guides, not guarantees. These are methods to give you the best chance at being successful in your negotiations.

As I wrote this book, it occurred to me that so much of this sounded like a game. The rules, some of them at least, are merely tools you can employ to help you successfully negotiate. Some people view buying a car as a competition; can I buy this SUV below cost? Can I walk away knowing that I have won and the dealership lost? Can I walk away knowing that the other person paid me way too much for my car? Conversely, if I paid more than I could have, if I wasn't able to wrestle another $500 off the price, I feel horrible – I drove away in my new Ford, but I lost! Shame on me.

This isn't a game, though. These rules are not intended to enforce your sense of victory and defeat. Rules II and III may be the very most important. Set your goals and know your topic. Your job is to walk away with an agreement that satisfies your needs, your goals, period. If you do that, you've won. Buying a car or a home, settling a labor dispute or obtaining a contract is not purely a competition, it's how we live and do business. You don't have to satisfy YOUR goals at the expense of others in order to succeed. You just have to satisfy your own goals, and you win.

Dana and Ted want to buy that Ford Edge for a price that they can afford and drive it home. If they do that, they win.

Jerry wants to sell Dana and Ted that Ford Edge today for a price that is OK with his boss. If he does that, he wins. These rules are designed to help put both of them in the best position to close the deal.

Another example. Some of those unfortunate homeowners who have been eaten alive by the subprime mortgage situation and real estate downturn played a game designed to let them buy a home that they could not afford. They forgot that their true goal should have been to buy a home that they could afford at a price they could handle, not to buy the biggest home any bank would allow them to. Some of them also gambled, something that you did not see in any of these rules and is antithetical to knowing the subject of your negotiation.

So don't let these rules turn you into a person on a mission to beat your negotiating partner. Approach these rules as suggestions for what to do in certain situations.

And never, ever look back. After you accept the offer, sign the papers, and drive your car home, forget about it. It is over. You will be able to find a better advertised price on a similar car, or home, it never fails. You will be able to find a seemingly comparable contract whose terms appear more favorable. It will happen. If you have done your homework and met your goal, it does not matter what the rest of the world could have done, or if someone else bought your SUV for less. This is not a competition. Enjoy your SUV.

CPSIA information can be obtained at www.ICGtesting.com
Printed in the USA
LVOW11*1412240715

447529LV00004B/6/P